Answer Key

for 100 Bible Stories and 100 Bible Stories Activity Book Revised Edition

CONCORDIA PUBLISHING HOUSE · SAINT LOUIS

Answer Key for

One Hundred Bible Stories *For Reflection* Questions

Contents

The Old Testament

The Old Testament

Primeval History (? to about 2000 B.C.)

1. The Creation: The First to the Fourth Day. Genesis 1

For Reflection

1. What does the creation tell us about the Creator? ◆ Creation shows us that the God who created everything is awesome in power, majesty, and knowledge. He shows the greatest attention to detail; creation reflects the power He imparted to it.
2. What evidence of the effects of sin do you see in the natural world around you? ◆ Nature is plagued with cruelty, destruction, pollution, storms, and drought.
3. Another way God showed His power was in sending Jesus to live, die, and rise again for the sins of the world. How can we show our love for Jesus in the way we care for all things He has made for us? ◆ We can look to preserve, conserve, and rightly manage all of God's creation as one way of living our life for Him, who died for us and rose again.

2. The Creation: The Fifth to the Seventh Day. Genesis 1

For Reflection

1. List several ways God has blessed you through the animals He has made. ◆ Answers will vary. Animals provide us with friendship, amusement, and sustenance of our environment. They also provide food, clothing, and other items for our welfare and benefit.
2. People are the creation God loved the most. He loved us so much that He sent Jesus to be our Savior and Friend. What special work does God give us to do for His honor and glory? ◆ God desires people to be fruitful and multiply, to subdue and rule over creation, and to proclaim the Gospel of salvation everywhere.
3. How do people show their love for God in the way they regard the day of rest set aside by Him? ◆ God's people show their love for God by obeying Him with regard to the day of rest, a day set aside by God as a time for physical and spiritual refreshment.

3. Adam and Eve in Paradise. Genesis 2

For Reflection

1. In what special way did God make the first man? the first woman? ◆ God formed the first man from the dust of the ground and breathed into his nostrils the breath of life. God made Eve from the rib of Adam.
2. Explain why marriage is a gift of God. ◆ God planned for a man and a woman to enjoy a special companionship in marriage—a one-flesh union in which each regards the other as an extension of himself or herself.
3. God gave Adam and Eve work to do in the Garden. How can we do our work in ways that show our love for Jesus? ◆ We can show our love for God by doing our work faithfully and competently, working for God Himself (Ephesians 6:6–7).

4. The Fall into Sin. Genesis 3

For Reflection

1. What consequences have come to you and to those around us as the result of Adam and Eve's sin? ◆ Sickness, death, persecution, and hardships of various kinds are all the result of sin.

2. How does the devil tempt us today? How has Jesus overcome sin and temptation for us? ◆ The devil tempts us to abandon Jesus for the desires and seduction our sinful world readily provides. Jesus faced and overcame temptation in our place and on our behalf.

3. After Adam and Eve sinned, they hid from God. Because we know Jesus as our Savior, we need never hide from God. What can we do instead? ◆ Instead of hiding from God, we can approach His throne of grace as His children, confident of His love and mercy.

5. The Promise of the Savior. Genesis 3

For Reflection

1. What consequences of sin fell upon Eve? Adam? the serpent? ◆ Eve would experience pain in childbirth. She would have to submit to her husband's leadership. Adam would know God's curse upon the ground; he would experience pain and troubles in his attempt to provide for his family. The serpent would have to crawl on the ground. (Apparently prior to the fall into sin, the serpent had legs.)

2. God told the serpent that the child of the woman would crush the head of the serpent. What did Jesus do to crush the head of Satan? ◆ Jesus crushed Satan's head by defeating Him through His death on Calvary's cross for the sins of all people. The resurrection was the completion of the victory.

3. What does it mean to you that Jesus has defeated the power of the devil? ◆ Jesus' defeat of the power of the devil means our freedom from the condemnation of sin.

6. Cain and Abel. Genesis 4

For Reflection

1. Why do you suppose God told Cain, "Sin is crouching at your door; it desires to have you, but you must master it"? ◆ God warned Cain about sin and its encroaching influence in his life.

2. How did God show His grace to Cain? How does He show His grace to us? ◆ God protected Cain by placing a mark on him so that he would not be killed. God protected us by sending Jesus to be our Savior. By faith we are marked for salvation in Him (see also Galatians 6:17).

3. How can we show our love and trust in Jesus as our Savior in the way we treat our brothers, sisters, and friends? in the way we treat all others? ◆ We can show our love for Jesus by treating all others, especially those closest to us, with the kind of selfless acts of love Jesus demonstrated toward us.

7. From Adam to Noah. Genesis 5

For Reflection

1. Calling on the name of the Lord refers to public worship. During whose lifetime did public worship begin? ◆ Public worship began during the lifetime of Seth, the son born to Adam and Eve among whose descendants the Savior of the world would be born.
2. Why is it a privilege to "call on the name of the Lord" in public worship? ◆ God's welcome of our praises and petitions shows His love for us and for all people through Christ, our Lord.
3. Enoch went to heaven without dying. The Bible says he "walked with God." Because of Jesus we need not be afraid of death. Explain. ◆ Death can claim no lasting hold on those who trust in Jesus. He will go with us "through the valley of the shadow of death" (Psalm 23:4).

8. The Flood. Genesis 6–9

For Reflection

1. What does the Flood remind us about God's attitude toward sin? ◆ God is just; He punishes sin.
2. The rainbow reminds us that God keeps His promise. What promise came true when Jesus was sent to earth to live, die, and rise again? ◆ God's promise to Adam and Eve and to their descendants to send a Savior from sin was kept in Jesus.
3. How does Noah's ark symbolize the church? ◆ Just as God saved Noah and his family in the ark, God saves His people through the means of grace, which He has given to His church.

9. The Tower of Babel. Genesis 11

For Reflection

1. Why did the people want to build a tower? ◆ In their self-focused pride they wanted to make a name for themselves by building a tower that would reach to the heavens.
2. How did the many languages of the world come into being? ◆ God instantly gave the people a multitude of languages so they could no longer understand one another and work well together.
3. God became angry with the people for trying to make a name for *themselves*, by their own doing. What name has God given us, by His doing? ◆ God has given us the name of Christ, or the designation of Christian—those who belong to God by faith in His Son, Jesus.

The Patriarchs (about 2000 to 1800 B.C.)

10. The Call of Abram. Genesis 12

For Reflection

1. How did Abraham show he loved God in the way he treated Lot? ◆ He was unselfish in his treatment of Lot.
2. When God told Abraham that all people would be blessed through him, God was

referring to Jesus, who would be born as a descendant of Abraham. How are all people blessed through Jesus? ◆ Jesus came to save all people from their sins. He desires that all people be saved.

3. In what ways can you bless others because you know Jesus as your Savior? ◆ Each of us can show our love for God in the unselfish way we deal with others. We can tell them of God and His love for us and for all people through Jesus.

11. The Promise of Isaac. Genesis 18

For Reflection

1. Who were Abraham's visitors? Why did Sarah laugh at their message? ◆ Abraham's visitors were the Lord and two angels (see footnote). Sarah did not believe the visitors' message.

2. Abraham shared a special meal with the Lord and the angels. What special meal do God's people share as part of a worship service? What makes this meal so special? ◆ God's people today share the Lord's Supper—the Sacrament of the Altar. In this meal participants receive the very body and blood of Christ in, with, and under the bread and wine.

3. Is anything too hard for the Lord? Why or why not? ◆ God is almighty; nothing is too hard for Him to do.

12. Sodom and Gomorrah. Genesis 19

For Reflection

1. Even in the act of destroying the wicked cities of Sodom and Gomorrah, God was at work saving His people. Explain. ◆ God sent His angels to rescue Lot and his family.

2. How does God protect you from evil? ◆ Similarly, God sends His holy angels to guard and protect us from evil.

3. The destruction of Sodom and Gomorrah reminds us of the final destruction awaiting all the wicked. Why can all who trust in Jesus as their Savior look forward to their eternal future with confidence? ◆ Jesus has defeated sin, death, and the devil's power. All who love and trust in Him need not fear the curse of hell. Instead Jesus will take us to live with Him forever in the happiness and bliss of heaven.

13. The Offering of Isaac. Genesis 22

For Reflection

1. What did Abraham show about his love for God in his willingness to sacrifice his son? ◆ Abraham demonstrated that his love for God superceded even that which he felt for his son.

2. Which other Father willingly allowed His Son to give His life as a sacrifice? What does this sacrifice mean to you? ◆ Our heavenly Father allowed His only Son to suffer and die for us and for our salvation.

3. Tell what it means to fear, love, and trust God above all things. ◆ By the power of the Holy Spirit, God's people love and honor God as the number one priority in their lives.

14. Isaac and His Family. Genesis 27

For Reflection

1. Why were the actions of Rebekah and Jacob wrong? ◆ They sought to obtain through trickery that which God had already planned for Jacob to receive (see Genesis 25:23).

2. What does Jesus' life, death, and resurrection mean for us when we feel sorrow over our own lies and dishonest acts? ◆ Jesus has earned forgiveness for these and all other sins.

3. As children of God, we also receive blessings from our Father. What blessings have we received from Him? How have we received them? ◆ As God's children through faith in Christ Jesus, we receive forgiveness of sins, new life, and eternal salvation at the hand of our loving and gracious God.

15. Jacob's Stairway. Genesis 28

For Reflection

1. One sin often leads to another. Jacob tricked his brother out of his blessing. How did Esau respond? ◆ Esau responded with threats of murder against Jacob.

2. Why do you think God gave Jacob the dream of the stairway to heaven with angels ascending and descending on it? ◆ God wanted Jacob to know of His ongoing love and care for him in spite of his sinfulness. God also wanted Jacob to know that He alone provides the way to heaven.

3. Jesus is the Son of God and Son of Man, on whom the angels ascend and descend. Explain. ◆ Jesus came to earth to close the separation that existed in the relationship between God and man (see John 1:51 and 1 Timothy 2:5).

16. Jacob's Family. Genesis 37

For Reflection

1. How was Joseph regarded by his father? by his brothers? Why did they regard him as they did? ◆ Joseph was his father's favorite son. Recognizing their father's favoritism, Joseph's brothers hated him.

2. What relationships trouble and concern you? What does Jesus' life, death, and resurrection mean to you as you think about those relationships? ◆ Answers to the first question will vary. Jesus' forgiveness and salvation provide us with the power to heal broken relationships.

3. Just as Joseph was Jacob's favorite child, we are favored in God's eyes. God gives us a "richly ornamented robe" too. (See verse in "Words to Remember.") What does this mean? ◆ Each person who belongs to God through faith in Jesus can say, "I delight greatly in the LORD; my soul rejoices in my God. For He has clothed me with garments of salvation and arrayed me in a robe of righteousness" (Isaiah 61:10).

17. Joseph and His Brothers. Genesis 37

For Reflection

1. Jacob's sons tricked him into thinking Joseph had been killed by a wild animal. Jacob had at one time also tricked his father. Recall the incident. ◆ At his mother's

direction, Jacob once disguised himself as his brother Esau and stole the birthright blessing his father intended to give to his brother.

2. The evil thoughts of Joseph's brothers led to evil actions. Explain. ◆ The brothers' evil thoughts against Joseph moved them to sell their brother into slavery and to lie to their father about what had happened to Joseph.

3. Reuben intercedes for Joseph and saves his life. Who has interceded for our lives? How? ◆ Jesus continues to intercede on our behalf to His Father in heaven. He opened the way for this intercession by living a perfect life and dying an atoning death in our place (see Romans 8:34).

18. Joseph Serves Pharaoh. Genesis 41

For Reflection

1. What dreams did Pharaoh dream? How did Joseph interpret them? ◆ Pharaoh dreamed of seven ugly cows swallowing seven healthy cows and of seven thin kernels of grain swallowing up seven healthy kernels of grain. By the power of God Joseph interpreted both dreams as containing the same meaning: seven years of famine would follow seven years of abundance.

2. Joseph told Pharaoh that God would give him an answer of peace. How does Jesus bring peace to all who love and trust in Him? ◆ Through the forgiveness, new life, and salvation Jesus won for us on Calvary, Jesus gives us the peace that passes all human understanding (Philippians 4:7).

3. God blessed Joseph abundantly. How does God abundantly bless all believers in Christ Jesus? ◆ Through Jesus, God gives us gifts of forgiveness, strength for daily life, and a home in heaven that no one can take from us.

19. The Journeys of Joseph's Brothers. Genesis 42–43

For Reflection

1. What occurrence astonished the brothers at the meal to which Joseph had invited them? ◆ Joseph seated his brothers according to their birth order.

2. How had Judah assured Jacob regarding the safety of Benjamin? ◆ Judah told Jacob he would be personally responsible for the welfare of Benjamin.

3. How has Jesus taken personal responsibility for us before our Father in heaven? ◆ Jesus has assumed the responsibilities to rescue and save us.

20. Joseph Makes Himself Known to His Brothers. Genesis 44–45

For Reflection

1. Judah volunteered to serve as a substitute for Benjamin. How does Judah remind us of Jesus? ◆ Jesus became our substitute, living a holy life and dying the death we deserved in order to save us.

2. Joseph made himself known to his brothers, adding that God was working in the events that had occurred to save their lives. Explain. ◆ Joseph said, "It was to save lives that God sent me ahead of you."

3. How does God make Himself known to us? Why is it important that He does? ◆ In order to bring us to faith so that we may be saved and live with Him forever, God has revealed Himself to us through His Word.

21. Jacob and Joseph Are Reunited. Genesis 46–50

For Reflection

1. What were Joseph's brothers afraid of after the death of their father? ◆ Joseph's brothers feared that after their father's death, Joseph would punish them for their cruelty to him.

2. Why are those who trust in Jesus as their Savior able to forgive others? ◆ God enables His followers in Christ Jesus to forgive others as God in Christ has forgiven them (Ephesians 4:32).

3. Read the verse in "Words to Remember." How did God work for good in Joseph's life? How does He work for good in our lives? ◆ God used the evil in Joseph's life to save His people. Somewhat similarly, God uses the evil that came to Jesus in His crucifixion ultimately to save us.

Moses and the Giving of the Law (about 1500 B.C.)

22. The Birth of Moses. Exodus 1–2

For Reflection

1. Moses' mother saved Moses by placing him in a small boat—a basket coated with tar and pitch so that it would float. Compare Moses and Noah. ◆ God used floating vessels to save both Noah and Moses.

2. How did God protect Moses from danger? How does He protect us? ◆ God protected Moses through the government of Egypt in allowing Moses to be found by Pharaoh's daughter. Among the ways God protects us is through the laws of our government. His greatest protection for us comes through Jesus' salvation. The protecting power of God also comes to us through His holy angels.

3. Moses was delivered from danger as a baby in order to "save" God's people from slavery in Egypt. What other baby was born to save His people? How did He save us? ◆ Jesus was born a baby; He came to save all people by living a holy life and dying an atoning death for all people everywhere.

23. The Call of Moses. Exodus 3–4

For Reflection

1. Of what did God remind Moses when he asked, "Who am I, that I should go to Pharaoh and bring the Israelites out of Egypt?" ◆ God reminded Moses of God's continual presence with him.

2. How did God equip and bless Moses for the work He had called him to do? ◆ God provided Moses with special signs and with the help and aid of his brother Aaron.

3. What gifts has God given to you to help you in your life? ◆ God provides His people today with the Sacraments of Baptism and the Lord's Supper and with the help, support, and encouragement of our brothers and sisters in the faith.

24. The Passover. Exodus 11–12

For Reflection

    1. What was the Passover? ◆ On the night before the departure of God's people from Egypt, the angel of death passed over the houses of Egypt, bringing death to those households not protected with the blood of the lamb.

    2. What were the Israelites to do on the evening before the Passover? ◆ They were to eat roasted meat with bitter herbs and bread made without yeast; they were to eat it in haste and be ready to leave on a journey.

    3. Why is Jesus called our Passover lamb? ◆ Jesus shed His blood for the salvation of all people.

25. The Departure from Egypt. Exodus 12–14

For Reflection

    1. What visual reminder of His presence among them did God give to His people? ◆ God led His people, providing a pillar of cloud to guide them by day and a pillar of fire to direct them at night.

    2. God's salvation of His people during the exodus from Egypt points to the even more dramatic rescue God later provided all people in Jesus. Tell about how Jesus rescued you at Calvary. ◆ Jesus allowed Himself to be nailed to a cruel Roman cross to pay for all of the sins of every person who ever lived or who ever will live.

    3. Are there times when you feel like you're caught between the Egyptian army and the Red Sea? Why need you not be afraid? ◆ Responses to the first question will vary. God is with us. Our loving Savior has promised never to leave us (Matthew 28:20).

26. The Giving of the Law. Exodus 15–16; 19–20

For Reflection

    1. God demonstrated His presence with smoke, fire, and the trembling of the mountain. How does God come to us today? ◆ God comes to us today through His Word and the Sacraments.

    2. Moses went up the mountain to speak with God on behalf of the people. In what way does Jesus speak to God on our behalf? ◆ Jesus forever intercedes with His Father in heaven on our behalf (Hebrews 7:25), reminding His Father that He has taken our sins upon Himself and paid their penalty in full.

    3. God sent manna and quail to help the Israelites by giving them food. He helped them by giving them the Law. Explain. ◆ God's Law tells us how it is best for us to live. God gave His commandments out of His amazing, unending love.

27. The Golden Calf. Exodus 32; 34

For Reflection

    1. The people of Israel had time on their hands as they waited for Moses to come down from the mountain. How did they misuse their time? ◆ They made an idol and began to worship it in place of the true and living God.

    2. What other gods do we sometimes worship? ◆ We sometimes worship the gods of popularity, possessions, and activities that take the place of the worship of the one true God.

3. Because of Jesus, why do we need not fear punishment for breaking the commandments? ◆ Jesus has paid the penalty for all sins.

28. The Bronze Snake. Numbers 13–14; 21

For Reflection

1. How did Joshua and Caleb show their trust in God? ◆ They expressed their trust in the ability of God to give the new land to them. They also warned others against rebelling against God.
2. What happened because the people, except Joshua and Caleb, refused to trust in God? ◆ Only those under 40 years of age were eventually permitted to enter the Promised Land. God sent venomous snakes among the people.
3. How is Jesus like the bronze snake the Lord told Moses to lift up to save the Israelites? ◆ Like the snake, Jesus was lifted up between heaven and earth so that all who believe in Him could have eternal life (John 3:14–15).

The Occupation of Canaan (about 1460 B.C.)

29. Israel Enters Canaan. Deuteronomy 34; Joshua 1–5

For Reflection

1. God told Joshua, "Be strong and courageous. Do not let this Book of the Law depart from your mouth; meditate on it day and night." Apply God's words to your life. ◆ As we study God's Word, His Spirit strengthens and encourages us. Therefore, God invites us to make frequent and regular use of His Word both alone and as we receive it in the Sacraments.
2. In what ways did God demonstrate His loving presence and care for His people? ◆ God miraculously provided for His people so that they could cross the Jordan and enter the Promised Land walking on dry ground. He also provided them with the produce of the land so that they no longer required manna for food.
3. The name *Joshua* means "The Lord saves." Share how Jesus has saved you and now gives you courage as you live for Him. ◆ Jesus saved us by living a holy life and by dying in our place for our sins. Knowing His forgiving, empowering, eternal love we can boldly face all that comes to us in life.

30. The Conquest of Canaan. Joshua 6–10

For Reflection

1. List the miracles God performed to help His people. ◆ God miraculously brought the walls of Jericho to the ground; He confused Israel's enemies and sent hailstones upon them; He stopped time so that the battle might continue in the light of day.
2. How did God keep the promise He made to the people of Israel? ◆ God gave the land to His people just as He had promised.
3. How has God kept His promises to you? ◆ God saves us through Jesus, just as He promised. One day He will bring us to the promised land of heaven.

The Time of the Judges (about 1440 to 1100 B.C.)

31. Gideon. Judges 6

For Reflection

1. Why did the people of Israel cry out to the Lord? ◆ They cried out to the Lord for help; they were under the rule of the Midianites.
2. For what reason did God want only 300 soldiers to go into battle against the Midianites? ◆ God knew that unless only a few soldiers were given victory, Israel would boast that they had won the victory by their own might.
3. Read the verse in "Words to Remember." After reading the story of Gideon, how do we know this passage is true? ◆ God always has our best interests foremost in mind.

32. Samson: Part 1. Judges 13–14

For Reflection

1. How do we know that God had a plan for Samson even before he was born? ◆ Before his birth God said of him, "He will begin the deliverance of Israel from the hands of the Philistines."
2. Explain Samson's riddle and its meaning. Samson's riddle: "Out of the eater, something to eat; out of the strong, something sweet." ◆ Meaning: Samson had killed a lion. Later he found that a swarm of bees had deposited honey inside the carcass.
3. How do we know that God was with Samson? How do we know He is with us? ◆ God's Spirit came upon Samson, providing him with great power. God's Spirit comes to us through Word and Sacrament, giving us faith, strength, and power to live as the children of God.

33. Samson: Part 2. Judges 15–16

For Reflection

1. What evidence can you give that Samson possessed great strength? ◆ Ropes fell from Samson's arms as if they were charred flax; he once killed a thousand men with the jawbone of a donkey.
2. How did Samson lose his great strength? ◆ Samson gave in to his unbelieving wife, who shaved his head.
3. What was the real source of Samson's strength? What is the source of our strength? ◆ God's Spirit was the source of Samson's strength. God's Spirit brings people to— and sustains us in—the one true faith.

34. Ruth. The Book of Ruth

For Reflection

1. What might have made it difficult for Ruth to go with her mother-in-law to live in Bethlehem? ◆ Ruth was from another culture than her mother-in-law. She would leave behind her family and friends, never to see them again.
2. Many years later, Jesus would be born to a descendant of Ruth. How does Ruth's background remind us that Jesus came to be the Savior of all people? ◆ As true

man, Jesus, the world's Savior, descended from Jewish as well as other people groups. He came to be the Savior of all (2 Corinthians 5:15).

3. Ruth's words to Naomi—"Where you go I will go, where you stay I will stay"—are considered to be the ultimate example of friendship. What meaning do these words have when coming from our ultimate Friend? ◆ Jesus promises to go and remain with us wherever we go throughout our life (Hebrews 13:5).

35. The Boy Samuel. 1 Samuel 1–4

For Reflection

1. How did Hannah show her gratefulness to God for the son He had given her? ◆ Hannah dedicated her son to the Lord and His lifelong service.
2. Eli had spoiled his sons. He did not discipline them for their sins. What was the result? ◆ Eli's sons disobeyed and turned their backs on God.
3. God spoke to Eli. How does God speak to us today, telling us of our sin and of Jesus as our Savior from sin? ◆ God speaks to His people today through His Word, Law and Gospel, recorded for us by the holy writers through the inspiration of the Holy Spirit.

The Undivided Kingdom (about 1100 to 975 B.C.)

36. King Saul. 1 Samuel 8–15

For Reflection

1. Why was Samuel displeased at the people of Israel's desire for a king? ◆ The people had rejected God as their King.
2. What did Saul do in disobedience to God? ◆ Instead of destroying the Ammonites and their possessions, Saul saved some of the animals to use in sacrifice.
3. Jesus desires to be King of our lives. What does Jesus, our King, invite us to do when we recognize that we have sinned? ◆ Jesus invites us to repent of our sin and to trust in the forgiveness He freely offers.

37. David Is Chosen. 1 Samuel 16–17

For Reflection

1. Describe the evil Goliath and the threat he posed to the people of Israel. ◆ Goliath chose himself to be the fighter in a one-on-one battle between the forces of evil and those of the true and living God.
2. We all have evil that threatens us and the lives we desire to live for Jesus. Give an example of some "Goliaths" you face. ◆ Examples will vary; they will include influences of the world, our sinful flesh, and the devil in our life and in the lives of those around us.
3. The Israelites, on hearing Goliath's threatening words, were terrified. Why can we be like David, and live without fear? ◆ Jesus has already won the victory for us over all that would finally destroy us. Nothing can separate us from His love (Romans 8:38–39).

38. David and Goliath. 1 Samuel 17

For Reflection

1. Why was David able to defeat the giant Goliath? ◆ God worked the victory.
2. What words of David show that he gave God the glory for his victory over Goliath, rather than seeking praise for himself? ◆ David said, "You come against me with sword and spear and javelin, but I come against you in the name of the LORD Almighty, the God of the armies of Israel. This day the LORD will hand you over to me, and the whole world will know that there is a God in Israel."
3. What "giants" has Jesus overcome for you? What "giants" has Jesus enabled you to overcome? ◆ Examples will vary. God promises us victory over all that would come against us (Isaiah 54:17).

39. David's Fall and Repentance. 2 Samuel 11–12

For Reflection

1. How did David respond when Nathan confronted him with his sin? ◆ David said, "As surely as the LORD lives, the man who did this deserves to die!"
2. After David admitted his sin, what did Nathan say to him? ◆ Nathan said, "The LORD has taken away your sin. You are not going to die."
3. We deserve to die because of our sins. What has Jesus done for us that makes it possible for us to be forgiven instead? ◆ Jesus died in our place to pay in full the penalty we deserved because of our sins.

40. Absalom's Rebellion. 2 Samuel 14–18

For Reflection

1. How did Absalom sin against his father? ◆ By fooling people and by force, Absalom sought to take his father's kingdom from him.
2. In what ways have you rebelled against your parents? against your Father in heaven? ◆ As sinners we regularly sin against our parents and against our heavenly Father. Specific examples will include sins of thought, word, and deed.
3. David cried over his rebellious son Absalom and wished he could have died in his place. What did our heavenly Father do for us in our rebellion against Him? ◆ God sent His only Son to die in our place so that our relationship with our Father in heaven might be restored.

41. Solomon and the Temple. 1 Kings 3–8

For Reflection

1. How did Solomon evidence his faith in the request he made of God? ◆ Instead of asking God for something for his own benefit or pleasure, Solomon asked God to make him a wise and discerning ruler of God's people.
2. The glory of the Lord filled the temple Solomon had made. In what way does the glory of the Lord fill our churches when God's people gather there for worship? ◆ The glory of God's presence evidences itself in the words that are spoken, read, and sung and received in the Sacraments.
3. Why does God, who, in Solomon's words, can't be contained by the highest heaven,

listen to our prayers? ◆ God listens to our prayers because of Jesus, who came to earth to live as one of us in order to earn our salvation.

The Divided Kingdom (about 975 to 588 B.C.)

42. The Prophet Elijah. 1 Kings 16–17

For Reflection

1. In what ways did God provide for His servant Elijah? ◆ God sent ravens to bring food to Elijah in the morning and evening at the Kerith Ravine; later God sent the widow of Zarephath to care for Elijah's needs.

2. How did God show His power over death? What does Jesus' victory over death mean for us as the children of God? ◆ God showed His power over death by returning the widow's son to life. Jesus' victory over death means that God will also one day raise our bodies to life and give us a new and eternal home with Him in glory.

3. How does God help you in times of need or trouble? ◆ God gives us His Word to support, encourage, and direct us during our times of trouble and hardship. He also provides people, medicines, and other resources to help us.

43. Elijah and the Prophets of Baal. 1 Kings 18

For Reflection

1. What false god did the people worship in Elijah's day? In what false gods do we sometimes place our trust? ◆ In Elijah's day the people worshiped the god Baal. False gods people worship today include satanic arts and witchcraft, money and possessions, and friends and influence.

2. How did God show His power to the people of Elijah's day? How did Jesus show His power over sin and evil? ◆ God sent a supernatural fire from heaven to consume the altar and its sacrifice. Jesus took our sins to the cross and displayed His victory over sin, death, and the devil in His resurrection.

3. Elijah alone defended the true God. When are we called to take an unpopular stand because of our faith in Jesus? ◆ Answers will include situations when our faith in Jesus requires us to stand alone against more popular, unbiblical perspectives and beliefs.

44. Naboth's Vineyard. 1 Kings 21

For Reflection

1. Ahab coveted the property of Naboth. Tell how coveting led Ahab and Jezebel to commit other sins. ◆ Ahab and Jezebel conspired wrongfully to convict and execute Naboth.

2. What can we learn from this story about the consequences of sin? ◆ One sin usually leads to other sins, often escalating in severity.

3. In the New Testament, another innocent man was put to death so that an undeserved inheritance might be claimed by many—including you and me. Explain. ◆ Though innocent, Jesus was put to death so that we might inherit the blessings of forgiveness, new life, and salvation, which our gracious God freely offers through Him.

45. Elisha Sees Elijah Ascend. 2 Kings 2

For Reflection

1. What did Elisha ask of Elijah? ◆ Elisha asked for a double portion of Elijah's spirit.
2. How did Elijah go to heaven? ◆ A chariot and horses of fire appeared, and Elijah was carried to heaven in a whirlwind.
3. How does God's Spirit come to—and work in—the lives of God's people today? ◆ God's Spirit comes to—and works in—the lives of God's people through the Word and the Sacraments—the means of grace.

46. Naaman and Elisha. 2 Kings 5

For Reflection

1. How did the young girl in this story share God's love with those who held her captive? ◆ She told her mistress about the help available through God's prophet in Samaria.
2. How was Naaman cured of his leprosy? ◆ Elisha told Naaman to wash seven times in the Jordan River. When Naaman did this, he was cured.
3. How are we "cured" of the disease of sin? ◆ We are washed in the blood of Jesus (see Revelation 7:14).

47. God Sends Jonah. Jonah 1–3

For Reflection

1. Why did Jonah run away from the Lord? ◆ Jonah did not want to go to Nineveh and preach against their wickedness as God had commanded him.
2. How did God show His kindness to Jonah in spite of Jonah's disobedience? ◆ After the sailors threw Jonah overboard, God rescued him by providing a great fish to swallow him and eventually bring him to land.
3. Jesus came to earth to die for our sins, earning our salvation for us. How does Jesus' death and resurrection compare to Jonah's experience inside the great fish? ◆ Just as Jonah was in the belly of the fish for three days and nights, Jesus was in the tomb and rose from the dead on the third day.

48. Jeremiah. Jeremiah 37–38

For Reflection

1. Why was Jeremiah thrown in the cistern? ◆ Jeremiah was put into the cistern because the words from God he spoke were disheartening and discouraging.
2. Why did Ebed-Melech want to help Jeremiah? ◆ Ebed-Melech knew that Jeremiah would die if no one rescued him.
3. How has Jesus rescued you in your troubles? ◆ He freely offers forgiveness of sins, strength to live a new life, and eternal salvation.

49. The Three Men in the Fiery Furnace. Daniel 3

For Reflection

1. How did Shadrach, Meshach, and Abednego live out their faith in the one true God? ◆ These men refused to disobey or disown the one true God.

2. How did God save the three young men who trusted in Him? ◆ He provided an angel to protect them in the fiery furnace.
3. What temptations do you face to deny your faith in Jesus? In what ways does Jesus rescue you? ◆ Temptations may include opportunities to follow the crowd in dishonoring or denying Jesus. Jesus rescues us by forgiving our sins and restoring us as His new people.

50. Daniel in the Lions' Den. Daniel 6

For Reflection
1. Why did the administrators and other leaders work to find fault with Daniel? ◆ These leaders were jealous of Daniel and the favored position he enjoyed.
2. How did God protect Daniel? ◆ God sent an angel to shut the mouths of the lions.
3. Do you think Daniel was afraid? What support does God give us when we are put in scary situations? ◆ Answers will vary. We need not fear; Jesus will remain with us through whatever hardships or trials we must endure. Finally he will take us to live eternally with Him in heaven.

The New Testament

The Youth of Jesus (about 7 B.C. to A.D. 6)

51. A Message for Zechariah. Luke 1

For Reflection
1. Tell how God provided Zechariah with good news. Why was this good news so unusual? ◆ God sent the angel Gabriel to tell Zechariah that God had heard his prayer and that Zechariah and his wife, Elizabeth, were to have a son. This good news was unusual because both Zechariah and Elizabeth were well beyond childbearing age.
2. What did Gabriel tell Zechariah about John's role and mission in life? ◆ Gabriel said that John would "make ready a people prepared for the Lord."
3. What message of good news has the Lord brought to you? How can you "be sure" of it? ◆ God has brought to us the Good News that Jesus is our Savior. We can be sure of this Good News because it comes to us from God Himself through His Word.

52. The Announcement to Mary. Luke 1; Matthew 1

For Reflection
1. What was Gabriel's message to Mary? ◆ Gabriel told Mary that she would have a Son and that she was to name her Son Jesus. Jesus would be the long-awaited Messiah.
2. The angel of the Lord appeared to Joseph and told him to name Mary's baby Jesus (Matthew 1:21). What does the name Jesus mean? ◆ Jesus means "Savior."

3. One of the names given to Jesus is *Immanuel*, which means "God with us." How is Jesus "God with us"? ◆ God came to dwell with us in human form in the person of Jesus (Philippians 2:6–8).

53. The Birth of John the Baptist. Luke 1

For Reflection

1. Why were people surprised that Zechariah and Elizabeth named their baby John? ◆ No one among their relatives had that name.
2. When did Zechariah regain his speech? What did Zechariah say after he became able to talk? ◆ Zechariah regained his ability to speak immediately after he wrote, "His name is John." Zechariah praised God.
3. How has God redeemed His people, including you and me? ◆ Jesus, God's Son, bought us back from sin, death, and the devil's power, taking our sins upon Himself on the cross.

54. The Birth of Jesus. Luke 2

For Reflection

1. How did it happen that God's Son was born in Bethlehem when Mary and Joseph lived in Nazareth in Galilee? ◆ Mary and Joseph traveled to Bethlehem because the government required them to travel there as part of a census.
2. Jesus' first bed was a manger. What does that tell us about God's Son? ◆ Jesus was born in the humblest of circumstances. He came to save all people, including the poor and lowly.
3. Why does this simple story give Christians so much reason to rejoice? ◆ Christians rejoice because God sent His Son to earth; we can go with His Son to heaven.

55. Angels Announce the Savior's Birth. Luke 2

For Reflection

1. According to the message of the angels, for whom had the Savior come? ◆ The angel told the shepherds of "good news of great joy that will be for all people."
2. The angels announced to the shepherds the good news. How did the shepherds respond? ◆ The shepherds hurried to Bethlehem to find the newborn Savior.
3. What is your reaction to the news of Jesus' birth? Why? ◆ Answers are likely to reflect gratitude and appreciation at God's indescribable gift (2 Corinthians 9:15).

56. The Presentation of Jesus. Luke 2

For Reflection

1. For what purpose did Mary and Joseph bring Jesus to the temple? ◆ Mary and Joseph brought Jesus to the temple to present Him to the Lord and to offer a sacrifice.
2. Why did Simeon and Anna bless and thank the Lord? ◆ Simeon and Anna thanked and praised God for sending the Savior of the world.
3. Simeon said he could die "in peace." Because of Jesus, why can we have peace even at the point of death? ◆ Jesus promises to take all who love and trust in Him to an eternal home in heaven at the conclusion of our earthly life.

57. The Magi from the East. Matthew 2

For Reflection

1. How did King Herod learn the birthplace of the Savior? ◆ Herod learned about Jesus' birth in Bethlehem from the Wise Men who came to Jerusalem inquiring about where the newborn King might be found.
2. What does the coming of the Magi signify for persons who are not of Jewish descent? ◆ Jesus has come to be the Savior of people of all nations and backgrounds.
3. Why were the Magi "overjoyed" when they saw the star? Do we have the same reason? Why or why not? ◆ The star led them to the newborn King. Answers to the second question may vary. Everyone whom God has led to Jesus may well experience being overjoyed. Jesus is the most important person any of us will ever meet; He is our Savior and eternal friend.

58. The Escape to Egypt. Matthew 2

For Reflection

1. How did God take care of His Son? ◆ God directed Joseph to take his family to Egypt, where Jesus would be safe.
2. Why was Herod determined to find and kill Jesus? How did God guide the Magi to "outwit" Herod? ◆ Herod did not want anyone to threaten his position as king. God directed the Magi in a dream not to return to Herod, but to go home by another route.
3. By faith, we, too, are the children of God. How does God take care of us? ◆ God protects and guides us along life's way, shielding us from harm and reminding us of His love and care.

59. The Boy Jesus at the Temple. Luke 2

For Reflection

1. Why did Jesus' parents go to Jerusalem every year? ◆ Jesus' parents went to Jerusalem each year to celebrate the Feast of the Passover.
2. What do you think Jesus meant when He asked, "Didn't you know I had to be in My Father's house?" ◆ Jesus wanted Mary and Joseph to recognize Him as the Son of God.
3. Where can we find Jesus today? What does He say to us? ◆ Jesus comes to us through God's Word as it is spoken, read, and reflected upon either privately in devotions or in the company of other believers, as at church.

The Public Ministry of Christ (about A.D. 29 to 33)

60. The Baptism of Jesus. Matthew 3; Mark 1

For Reflection

1. Describe the appearance and work of John. ◆ John wore clothes of camel's hair with a leather belt. He preached repentance and baptized people in the Jordan.
2. The three Persons of the Trinity can be clearly identified at Jesus' Baptism. Explain.

◆ As Jesus, God's Son, was being baptized, God the Father spoke from heaven, and the Holy Spirit descended upon Jesus like a dove.

3. Jesus came to "fulfill all righteousness," or do God's will. This includes His death. Why did He have to die? (See verse in "Words to Remember.") ◆ Jesus took our sin upon Himself so that we might be given His righteousness.

61. The Temptation of Jesus. Matthew 4

For Reflection

1. What did Jesus use in response to the devil's temptation? ◆ Jesus used God's Word to fend off the temptations of the devil.
2. Jesus resisted the devil's power. What does this show us about Jesus? ◆ Jesus is stronger than the devil.
3. What does Jesus' victory over temptation mean for us in our daily Christian lives? ◆ Because Jesus overcame the devil's temptations, we also can face and overcome them by the power His Spirit provides (1 Corinthians 10:13).

62. Jesus Helps Peter Catch Fish. Luke 5

For Reflection

1. How did Jesus take care of the needs of the people? How does Jesus provide for our needs? ◆ Jesus first provided for people's spiritual needs, teaching them God's Word. Then He provided a miraculous catch of fish. Everything we have comes from our gracious God; He meets all of our needs through the blessings He provides.
2. How did Simon Peter react to Jesus after the miracle of the large catch of fish? ◆ Peter said, "Go away from me, Lord; I am a sinful man!"
3. What new direction in life did Jesus give to Simon Peter? What new direction does Jesus bring to our lives? ◆ Jesus called Peter to be one of His disciples. Somewhat similarly Jesus calls us to bring the Good News to those who do not yet believe.

63. Jesus Changes Water to Wine. John 2

For Reflection

1. Describe Jesus' first miracle. ◆ While Jesus and His disciples were guests at a wedding, Mary told Jesus that they had run out of wine. Mary told the servants to do whatever Jesus would tell them. Jesus told them to fill six large jars with water. He miraculously changed the water into wine.
2. According to the last verse of this account, what happened as a result of Jesus' miracles? ◆ Jesus revealed His glory, and the disciples put their faith in Him.
3. What does Jesus' ability to do miracles tell you about Him? ◆ Jesus is the Son of God.

64. Jesus Calms the Storm. Mark 4

For Reflection

1. How, in this account, does Jesus show Himself to be truly human? ◆ Jesus slept.

2. How, in this account, does Jesus show Himself to be true God? ◆ Jesus calmed the storm.

3. How does Jesus help us during the storms in our life? ◆ Jesus provides the calm assurance of His love and care even during the worst of storms.

65. Jesus Heals a Man Who Was Paralyzed. Mark 2

For Reflection

1. What criticism did Jesus receive when He forgave the sins of the paralyzed man? ◆ The teachers of the law thought that Jesus was blaspheming because only God can forgive sins.

2. By healing the paralyzed man, what did Jesus prove to those who criticized Him? ◆ Jesus proved Himself to be God and to be able to forgive sins.

3. Compare the help Jesus provided the paralyzed man with the help He gives to you. ◆ Although Jesus may not heal all bodily illnesses or disorders, Jesus forgives all sins including mine. He died for all sins at Calvary.

66. A Widow's Son and Jairus' Daughter. Luke 7–8

For Reflection

1. How do both of these events show that God feels our hurt when those we love die? ◆ Jesus' heart "went out to" the widow whose son had died. He helped both mourners, bringing both the young man and the girl back to life.

2. What other event shows Jesus' ultimate power over death? ◆ The raising of Lazarus and Jesus' own resurrection show His power over death.

3. What does it mean to you that Jesus brings back to life those who have died? ◆ Jesus will one day raise up to life eternal all who love and trust in Him.

67. Jesus Feeds More Than Five Thousand. John 6

For Reflection

1. What does the feeding of the multitude teach us about Jesus? ◆ Jesus cares about our physical as well as our spiritual needs and concerns.

2. What did those who witnessed the miracle conclude about Jesus? ◆ Those who witnessed the miracle said, "Surely this is the Prophet who is to come into the world."

3. In what ways does Jesus provide all your daily needs? ◆ Jesus gives us everything we need and have, including food, clothing, and shelter.

68. Jesus Walks on the Water. Mark 6; Matthew 14

For Reflection

1. Why do you suppose the people wanted Jesus to be their earthly king? ◆ The people thought they could force Jesus to provide miraculously for their physical needs without their having to work to provide for themselves.

2. In this account Peter shows himself as a man of faith and a man of doubt. Explain. ◆ Peter desired to walk on water; for a time he did so successfully. Peter also doubted when he saw the wind, and he began to sink before Jesus saved him.

3. Like Peter, we all have times when we doubt. How did Jesus help Peter when he doubted? How will Jesus help us? ◆ Jesus reached out His hand and caught Peter; Jesus, through His Word, reaches us and rescues us, strengthening our faith and encouraging us in our daily life of faith.

69. The Faith of a Canaanite Woman. Matthew 15

For Reflection

1. Why did Jesus' disciples want Him to send the Canaanite woman away? ◆ Because Jesus did not answer the woman, perhaps the disciples thought she was a nuisance to Him.

2. How did the prayer of the woman to Jesus indicate her great faith? ◆ The woman persistently asked Jesus for help for her daughter.

3. What can we learn from the story of the Canaanite woman about prayers offered on behalf of the welfare of others? ◆ The woman asked for healing for another (her daughter), and Jesus granted her request. We, too, can petition God on behalf of others.

70. The Ten Lepers. Luke 17

For Reflection

1. In what ways was life hard for the lepers? ◆ Lepers were required to live in isolation from others. They were often despised and extremely poor.

2. What motivated the one leper to return to Jesus? Why do you suppose the other nine lepers did not come back to Jesus? ◆ One healed man returned to Jesus to thank Him. Answers will vary. The point can be made that the nine were obeying Jesus, who told them to go and show themselves to the priests.

3. For what blessings can you thank Jesus today? ◆ Answers will vary but may include spiritual as well as material blessings.

71. Jesus Blesses the Children. Matthew 18–19

For Reflection

1. What did Jesus mean by the saying "unless you change and become like little children, you will never enter the kingdom of heaven"? ◆ Only those with faith in Jesus will be saved.

2. Some people have considered children as unimportant or nuisances. But what does Jesus say about the importance of children? ◆ Jesus said, "Their angels in heaven always see the face of My Father in heaven" (Matthew 18:10).

3. How did Jesus show His love for children? ◆ He took the children in His arms, put His hands on them, and blessed them.

72. The Transfiguration. Matthew 17

For Reflection

1. To be transfigured is to be changed. Describe Jesus' transfiguration. ◆ In the presence of Peter, James, and John, Jesus' face suddenly shone bright like the sun and His clothes became as white as the light. Moses and Elijah appeared in glorious splendor, talking with Jesus.

2. What topic did Jesus discuss with Moses and Elijah? ◆ They spoke about Jesus' coming sacrifice for the sins of the world.
3. What does it mean to you that Jesus is the Son of God? ◆ As the Son of God, Jesus is the promised Messiah, long-awaited by the prophets of old, and my personal Savior, who died for me and rose again.

73. Zacchaeus. Luke 19

For Reflection
1. What do we know about Zacchaeus? ◆ Zacchaeus was a chief tax collector, short in stature, and wealthy.
2. How did Zacchaeus show that he had become a follower of Jesus? ◆ He gave half of his possessions to the poor and promised to repay four times as much as he had cheated anyone.
3. How do you know that Jesus came to earth to save you? ◆ Answers will vary. We know of Jesus' salvation because someone has brought the message of God's Word—or God's Word itself—to us.

The Parables of the Savior (about A.D. 29 to 33)

74. The Lost Sheep and the Lost Coin. Luke 15

For Reflection
1. What criticism led Jesus to tell parables about the lost sheep and lost coin? ◆ The Pharisees and teachers of the law muttered, "This man welcomes sinners and eats with them."
2. What do the shepherd and the woman do in the stories? Why do they rejoice? ◆ They search diligently and persistently for that which is lost. They rejoice because the cherished lost item is recovered.
3. Are you one of the lost sheep our Shepherd came to find? Why or why not? ◆ Although those brought up in the faith may not recognize themselves as having been lost, each of us was lost according to our natural condition before Jesus found us through His Word.

75. The Lost Son. Luke 15

For Reflection
1. What words would you use to describe the father in the story? ◆ The father is loving, forgiving, seeking, and restoring.
2. Much like the lost son, we don't deserve to be called children of our heavenly Father. Why? ◆ We, too, have turned our backs on God and His grace and are not worthy, outside of the merits of Christ, to claim a place in His family.
3. What did our heavenly Father do for us so that we might live as His children? ◆ He sent His Son to earn the right for us to reenter God's family as His forgiven children.

76. The Foolish Rich Man. Luke 12

For Reflection

1. What sin does Jesus' story warn against? ◆ Jesus warns against all kinds of greed.
2. What does it mean to seek God's kingdom? ◆ To seek the kingdom of God means to live life as God's children, according to His will.
3. What does Jesus also promise to those who seek His kingdom? ◆ Jesus promises that those who seek God's kingdom will be blessed with the material things they need as well.

77. The Pharisees and the Tax Collector. Luke 18

For Reflection

1. Which of the two men evidenced faith in God, trusting in His grace and goodness for salvation? ◆ The humble tax collector acknowledged both his sinfulness and his trust in God with the simple words "God have mercy on me, a sinner."
2. How do we know that God listened to the prayer of the tax collector? ◆ Jesus said, "I tell you that this man, rather than the other, went home justified before God."
3. What Good News does God have for all who, burdened by sin, pray the prayer of the tax collector? ◆ Jesus welcomes sinners. He forgives all who come to Him bearing the burden of their sin (see John 6:37).

78. The Good Samaritan. Luke 10

For Reflection

1. Which words summarize the Law of God that Jesus lived in our place in order to earn heaven for us? ◆ "Love the Lord your God with all your heart and with all your soul and with all your strength and with all your mind" and "Love your neighbor as yourself."
2. Who is our neighbor? Give examples that show how to be a Christian neighbor. ◆ Everyone who needs our help is our neighbor. We show our love for Jesus by unselfishly giving of ourselves to others, especially to those in need.
3. Which of the characters in this story reminds us most of Jesus? Why? ◆ The Good Samaritan reminds us of Jesus' self-sacrificing work to redeem us. Jesus gave His very self to rescue and save us.

The Passion and Death of Christ (about A.D. 33)

79. The Triumphal Entry. Matthew 21

For Reflection

1. What Old Testament prophecy did Jesus fulfill in this account? ◆ Jesus fulfilled the Old Testament prophecy "Say to the Daughter of Zion, 'See, your king comes to you, gentle and riding on a donkey, on a colt, the foal of a donkey.' "
2. How did the people worship Jesus? ◆ They spread their cloaks and branches on the road in front of Him and shouted, "Hosanna to the Son of David! Blessed is He who comes in the name of the Lord! Hosanna in the highest!"

3. How and why do we worship Jesus today? ◆ We worship Jesus publicly in worship services and festivals. We worship Jesus privately in our devotions and prayers. In still another sense, we worship Jesus in lives lived to His glory.

80. The Anointing. Mark 14; John 12

For Reflection

1. Describe Mary's act of worship. ◆ Mary took a pint of pure nard, an expensive perfume, poured it on Jesus' feet, and wiped His feet with her hair.
2. What had Jesus done for Mary and her family? ◆ Jesus, friend and teacher of Mary and her siblings Martha and Lazarus, had raised Lazarus from the dead.
3. What good things has Jesus done for you and your family? ◆ Answers will vary. Jesus has given us all we have, including forgiveness of sins, new life, and salvation in His name.

81. The Last Judgment. Matthew 25

For Reflection

1. Who will come before Jesus and the holy angels on Judgment Day? ◆ All people, the living and the dead, will come before Jesus on the day of judgment.
2. By what evidence will Jesus identify those who have lived in faith in Him? ◆ Jesus will describe the good things His followers have done in faith for others who love and trust in Him.
3. The people on the King's right showed mercy to those less fortunate than they. How has Jesus shown mercy to us? ◆ Jesus has lived, suffered, and died to earn our salvation.

82. The Lord's Supper. Luke 22

For Reflection

1. Tell how Judas turned his back on Jesus. ◆ Judas turned his back on Jesus and the forgiveness He freely offered and instead took his own life.
2. Jesus and His disciples assembled to eat the Passover meal. Compare the Passover meal with the new meal Jesus gave to His followers. What does Jesus give us in the Lord's Supper? ◆ The Passover meal featured a lamb without defect; Jesus—holy and sinless—was such a "lamb." The Passover remembered the salvation God provided Israel when He freed them from bondage in Egypt; the Lord's Supper offers Christ's very body and blood together with the bread and wine for the forgiveness of sins Jesus earned on the cross.
3. Why did Jesus give His body and blood? How did He do it? ◆ Jesus gave His body and blood for us and for our salvation. He sacrificed Himself for us by dying a horrible death on a cross.

83. Jesus in Gethsemane. Matthew 26; Lukc 22

For Reflection

1. How does Jesus' prayer to His heavenly Father show Him to be true man? What evidence do you find in this account that Jesus is true God? ◆ Jesus began to be

deeply distressed and troubled, overwhelmed with sorrow to the point of death in anticipation of the agony about to begin. As true God Jesus was all-knowing. He knew the suffering He was about to endure. He also called God His Father.

2. What did Jesus ask His disciples to do? Why were they unable to do what He asked? ◆ Jesus asked His disciples to watch and pray. Although they desired to remain awake to watch and pray, they were physically exhausted and fell asleep.

3. Why was Jesus willing to submit to God's will, even though He knew the enormous pain and suffering He would have to endure? ◆ Jesus submitted to His Father's will in order to earn our forgiveness and eternal salvation by suffering and dying in our place (passive obedience).

84. Jesus Is Betrayed and Arrested. Matthew 26; John 18

For Reflection

1. Why do you suppose Judas was willing to betray Jesus? ◆ Judas was most likely motivated by money. Perhaps he thought Jesus would be arrested and then would escape the crowd as He had done in the past (Luke 4:28–30).

2. Why didn't Jesus call to His Father and ask for the assistance of angels? ◆ Jesus submitted to the arrest and subsequent humiliation, suffering, and death in order to earn our salvation.

3. How did Jesus show His love and care for the servant of the high priest? ◆ Jesus touched the man's ear and healed him.

85. Jesus before the Sanhedrin. Matthew 26; John 18

For Reflection

1. How does Jesus respond when asked whether He is the Christ, the Son of God? ◆ Jesus said, "Yes, it is as you say."

2. Jesus was accused of committing blasphemy. Who was actually guilty of committing blasphemy? ◆ The chief priests, members of the Sanhedrin, and the soldiers were actually the ones committing blasphemy by insulting and abusing the one true God in the person of Jesus.

3. If Christ was the Son of God, why did He endure the abuse at the hands of His opponents? ◆ Jesus willingly submitted to torture, pain, and death in order to save us.

86. Peter Disowns Jesus; Judas Dies. Matthew 26–27; Luke 22; John 18

For Reflection

1. Peter followed Jesus into the high priest's palace. Yet he denied knowing Jesus. Why? ◆ Peter was curious as to what was going on. Yet he feared association with someone who had been arrested and was standing trial.

2. Both Peter and Judas became sorry for what they had done. In what ways was their sorrow different? ◆ Whereas Peter turned to God in repentance, Judas sank into despair and turned away from God. Peter was reinstated as a disciple of Christ; Judas took his own life.

3. Because of our sinful nature, we, like both Peter and Judas, are guilty of betraying the Lord. Judas lost hope because of his guilt. Is there reason for us to lose hope?

Why not? ◆ No one need ever lose hope. Jesus died for all people. He offers His forgiveness, new life, and salvation to all people. No sin is too great for Him to forgive.

87. Jesus before Pilate. Matthew 27; John 18

For Reflection

1. Describe how Jesus suffered under Pontius Pilate. ◆ Under Pilate Jesus was mocked, humiliated, and tortured in an unsuccessful attempt on Pilate's part to gain the sympathy of the people for Jesus.
2. Why did Pilate sentence Jesus to be crucified even though he knew Jesus to be innocent? ◆ Pilate gave in to the will of the crowd, putting his desire to appease the masses above his desire to see justice done.
3. The people said to Pilate, "Let [Jesus'] blood be on us and on our children." What does it mean for believers to be covered with the blood of Christ? ◆ Jesus' blood has been shed so that we might have the forgiveness of sin (1 John 1:7).

88. Jesus Is Crucified. Luke 23; John 19

For Reflection

1. What do we learn about Jesus from the words He spoke on the cross? ◆ Jesus' words from the cross show His willingness to pray for others, to save others, and to be forsaken by God Himself for us and our salvation. They also show His concern for His mother.
2. What miraculous events occurred to indicate the significance of Jesus' death? ◆ Darkness covered the whole land for three hours, the temple curtain was torn in two, the earth shook, and people were raised to life.
3. What does it mean to you personally that Jesus died on a cross long ago on Calvary? ◆ Answers will vary, but are likely to include individual confessions of faith and expressions of gratitude for Jesus as the students' personal Savior.

89. Jesus Dies and Is Buried. Matthew 27; Luke 23; John 19

For Reflection

1. How did the soldier make sure that Jesus was indeed dead? ◆ He pierced Jesus' side.
2. Describe the burial of Jesus. ◆ Joseph of Arimathea, a prominent member of the Council, went to Pilate and boldly asked for Jesus' body. Together with Nicodemus, who brought a mixture of myrrh and aloes, he took Jesus' body, wrapped it, and placed it in a new tomb, rolling a stone in front of the entrance.
3. Why was it so important that Jesus physically die? (See "Words to Remember.") ◆ Jesus died so that we might be freed from the slavery of sin. Jesus' death was the price required to pay for our sins.

The Glorified Christ (about A.D. 33)

90. The Resurrection of Christ. Matthew 28; Mark 16

For Reflection

1. Tell about the actions of the angel on Easter morning. ◆ On Easter morning amidst a violent earthquake, the angel came to the tomb, rolled back the stone, and sat on it. The guards were so afraid of the angel that they shook and became like dead men. When the women came to the tomb, the angel (now inside the tomb) pronounced to them that Jesus had risen.
2. How did the women respond to the message of the angel? ◆ They hurried away from the tomb, afraid, yet filled with joy.
3. What does the message of the angel mean for us today? ◆ Jesus' resurrection is the foundation on which the Christian faith is built (see also 1 Corinthians 15:12–22).

91. The First Appearances of the Risen Lord. Matthew 28; John 20

For Reflection

1. Describe Jesus' first resurrection appearances. ◆ As the women ran to tell the disciples the angel's message, Jesus appeared to them, and they worshiped Him. Then Jesus appeared to Mary as she stood outside the tomb crying. Mary had not heard the angel's announcement. At first she thought Jesus was the gardener. She recognized Jesus when He spoke her name.
2. How did the leaders of the people attempt to "cover up" the good news of Jesus' resurrection? ◆ The chief priests and elders gave the soldiers a large sum of money to say that the disciples came during the night and stole Jesus' body while they were asleep.
3. Why are the appearances of Jesus after His resurrection so important? ◆ Jesus' appearances prove that He physically rose from the dead.

92. Christ Appears to His Disciples. John 20; Matthew 28

For Reflection

1. Jesus twice tells His disciples, "Peace be with you!" How is peace related to Christ's resurrection? ◆ Jesus' resurrection brings His followers peace in the assurance that our faith and the promises to which Christians cling are true and certain. In Jesus we have forgiveness, new life, and eternal salvation.
2. Why did Jesus invite the disciples to look at His hands and feet? ◆ Jesus wanted His disciples to be eyewitnesses to His bodily resurrection.
3. Jesus promised the disciples His power and His presence in the new life they were to live for Him. Describe the goals and objectives God brings to the lives of all who love and trust in Jesus the risen Savior. ◆ Jesus desires His people to bring the Good News of His salvation to all people. Jesus' followers witness to His power and presence by both word and example.

93. The Ascension. Acts 1

For Reflection

1. What gift did Jesus tell the disciples to wait for in Jerusalem? ◆ Jesus told them they would be baptized with the Holy Spirit.
2. What did the angels promise the disciples after Jesus ascended into heaven? ◆ The angels said, "This same Jesus, who has been taken from you into heaven, will come back in the same way you have seen Him go into heaven" (Acts 1:11).
3. Although Jesus ascended into heaven, He has not been "taken away" from us. Explain. ◆ Jesus remains with His people, just as He promised, even though we cannot see Him (Matthew 28:20).

The Church of Christ (about A.D. 33 to 60)

94. The Holy Spirit Comes at Pentecost. Acts 2

For Reflection

1. In what ways did the Holy Spirit make His presence known at Pentecost? ◆ The Holy Spirit came with a sound like the blowing of a violent wind, filling the house. Jesus' followers saw what seemed to be tongues of fire that separated and came to rest on each of them. Then the people began to speak in languages they had never learned.
2. Describe Peter's Pentecost sermon and its result. ◆ Peter preached a powerful sermon, telling those assembled about the life and death of the Son of God. In sorrow over their sins the people asked, "Brothers, what shall we do?" Peter replied, "Repent and be baptized, every one of you, in the name of Jesus Christ for the forgiveness of your sins. And you will receive the gift of the Holy Spirit." Those who accepted his message were baptized. That day over three thousand were added to the church.
3. In what ways does the Holy Spirit come to and work in the lives of God's people today? ◆ God converts people and keeps them alive in faith through the means of grace—God's Word and the Sacraments.

95. The Crippled Beggar Is Healed. Acts 3

For Reflection

1. Whom did Peter and John credit for the miraculous healing of the beggar?
   ◆ They healed the beggar in the name of Jesus Christ of Nazareth.
2. How did Peter use the healing of the beggar to tell others about Jesus? ◆ Peter clearly tells the people that Jesus' power healed the man. Then Peter tells them about Jesus' life and mission and how the people put Jesus to death. Peter invites the people to repent, and many came to faith.
3. The beggar asked for money and received healing instead. In what unexpected ways has God in Christ blessed you? ◆ Answers will vary somewhat but will focus on the most important gifts of forgiveness, new life, and salvation.

96. Stephen. Acts 6–8

For Reflection

1. Why was Stephen stoned to death? ◆ Stephen died for boldly professing his faith in Jesus.
2. What did Stephen pray as his enemies were killing him? Whose example was he following? ◆ Stephen prayed for those putting him to death, just as Jesus did. He said, "Lord, do not hold this sin against them."
3. Describe the strength of Stephen's faith. How does God's Spirit help those who believe in Jesus when they face ridicule and opposition? ◆ Stephen's faith was very strong; it enabled him to face persecution and death. Through Word and Sacrament God's Spirit offers the same power to all believers.

97. Philip and the Ethiopian. Acts 8

For Reflection

1. How did Philip meet the Ethiopian? ◆ An angel of the Lord directed Philip to go south to the desert road. Here Philip met the Ethiopian.
2. Explain the meaning of the passage the Ethiopian was reading. ◆ Jesus is the subject of Isaiah's prophecy. He was led like a sheep to the slaughter. Like a lamb before the shearer, Jesus also was silent. Jesus suffered humiliation and death so that we might be saved.
3. What reason do those who know Jesus as their Savior have for being joyful? ◆ Through His life, death, and resurrection, Jesus has solved our biggest problems. He has earned our freedom from sin, death, and Satan's power.

98. Saul's Conversion. Acts 9

For Reflection

1. Describe Saul before and after Jesus came to claim him as His own. ◆ The Holy Spirit changed Saul from a persecutor of Christians to a Christian missionary.
2. Saul was blind both before and after Jesus spoke to him. In what way were we like Saul in his blindness? In what way are we now able to see? ◆ Before we came to faith we, too, were blind—spiritually. Without faith we do not know God or desire Him and the salvation He offers.
3. What special work did Jesus have for Saul to do? What special work does He have for you to do? ◆ Jesus chose Saul to be His chosen instrument to bring the Gospel to the Gentiles. Students' answers are likely to reflect opportunities to serve God with individual talents, skills, and abilities.

99. Peter Is Freed from Prison. Acts 12

For Reflection

1. How did the members of the church respond after Peter was arrested? ◆ While Peter was in prison, the church was earnestly praying to God for him.
2. Why did Rhoda not let Peter into the house? ◆ When she recognized Peter's voice, she was so overjoyed she ran back to the assembly without opening the door for Peter.

3. For whom can you pray today? ◆ Answers might include those who are persecuted and imprisoned because of their faith in Jesus.

100. Paul's Shipwreck. Acts 27–28

For Reflection

1. Paul was arrested and was on his way to be tried in Rome because he believed in Jesus. Tell about the adventure he encountered along the way. ◆ While en route the ship on which Paul was traveling experienced a severe storm with winds of hurricane force. The storm raged for so many days that the passengers gave up all hope of being rescued. After an angel brought Paul an encouraging message, the ship ran aground, and all found safety on an island.

2. Why wasn't Paul worried though a severe storm raged on around him? ◆ Paul knew of God's plan for him.

3. Why can you have courage even as you face storms and troubles in your life? ◆ Like Paul we need not be afraid even in the midst of life's most severe storms because Jesus has a plan for us; one day we will live with Him in heaven.

Answers to One Hundred

Bible Stories Activity Book

Revised Edition

Contents

The Old Testament

1 The Creation: The First to the Fourth Day
(Genesis 1)

Thinking about God's Word

1. What word tells who created the world? **(the Bible)**

2. What is meant by "the beginning"? **(at the start of creation)**

3. Who lived before the beginning? **(God)**

4. Which words tell what happened every time God said, "Let there be"? **("there was; it was so")**

5. In what way does God continue to create the world today? **(God continues to populate His creation with plants, animals, and people. He preserves all He has made.)**

6. How was it possible for God to create all things out of nothing? **(With God all things are possible. God used His infinite power to create the world.)**

7. In John 1:1–3 the Son of God is called "the Word." What connection is there between "the Word" and "God said"? **(Jesus is God's Word made flesh. God's Word has power. Jesus proved His power and authority when He defeated sin, death, and Satan for us.)** Which persons of the Holy Trinity were active in the work of creation? **(All three persons, Father, Son, and Holy Spirit, were active in creation.)**

Working with God's Word

On the blank lines write on which day God created the following:

1. Sun, moon, and stars **4**

2. Day and night **1**

3. Earth and planets **1**

4. Land, trees, rivers and plants **3**

5. Sky and water **2**

Fill in the blanks.

1. In the beginning God **created** the heavens and the earth.

2. The earth was **formless** and empty.

3. God separated the light from the **darkness.**

4. God called the light **day.**

5. The darkness God called **night.**

6. God called the expanse **sky.**

7. God called the dry ground **land.**

8. Each day consisted of evening and **morning.**

Applying God's Word

1. Compare the world as God originally created it and the world in which we live. Note similarities and differences. **(The world, both before and after the fall, suggests the awesome power and majesty of the Creator. The perfection and harmony of the original creation was shattered by the fall into sin.)**

2. What do these first verses of Genesis 1 reveal to us about God? **(God existed before the beginning of time; He is powerful enough to create all things through His Word; everything God made was good.)**

3. What does God's Word accomplish as we receive it in the Sacraments? **(Through the Word the Holy Spirit works faith, giving people the blessings of forgiveness, eternal life, and salvation in Jesus.)**

2 The Creation: The Fifth to the Seventh Day
(Genesis 1)

Thinking about God's Word

1. How can you tell that the Creator made a large number of living creatures in the beginning? **(Plural forms are used in reference to the creatures God made. He said, "Let the waters teem with living creatures.")**

2. Which words show that God wanted the whole earth to be filled with living things? **("Be fruitful and increase in number.")**

3. Who is meant by "Us" and "Our" when God spoke about making people? **(the three persons of the Trinity—Father, Son, and Holy Spirit)**

4. How many human beings did God make on the sixth day? **(two—Adam and Eve)** Which words show that God wanted them to have children who in time would live all over the world? **("Be fruitful and increase in number; fill the earth and subdue it.")**

5. In what two ways did God say that people were to be rulers over the other creatures? **(People were to rule over all the earth and over all its creatures.)**

6. What was the chief difference between people and the other moving creatures? **(People were created in the image of God.)**

7. Which words tell that there was not a mistake or a flaw in anything God had made? **(It was good—"very" good.)**

8. How did God show on the seventh day that there was nothing more that He wanted to create? **(He rested.)**

9. Did God let the animals look out for themselves after He had created them? **(No, people are to care for animals.)** How does He still preserve and govern them? **(He gives them life, food, habitat, etc.)**

10. How does the picture try to show that there was peace and happiness among God's creatures? **(Creation is shown at peace; no predator/prey relationships are depicted.)**

11. Tell what God created on each day. Think of the wise plan God followed in what He made from day to day. **(The first three days are sometimes referred to as days of forming, and the last three days are sometimes referred to as days of filling. The light created on Day 1 is complemented with the lights created on Day 4. The separation of water under the expanse from water above it is complemented with the water creatures and winged birds God made in Day 5. The dry ground and vegetation God created on Day 3 were complemented with animals, and people made on Day 6.)**

Working with God's Word

On the blank lines write on which day God created the following:

1. Man **6**
2. Cats **6**
3. Turtles **6**
4. Deer **6**
5. Sharks **5**
6. Cows **6**
7. Whales **5**
8. Worms **6**
9. Chickens **6**
10. Ants **6**

Fill in the blanks.

1. God said, "Let birds fly above the **earth** across the expanse of the sky."
2. God blessed them and said, "Be fruitful and **increase** in number."
3. Birds and water animals were made on the **fifth** day.
4. God said, "Let Us make man in Our **image**, in Our likeness."
5. So God created man in His own **likeness**.
6. Male and **female** He created them.
7. God told them, "Fill the earth and **subdue** it."

8. On the sixth day God created animals and **people**.

9. Everything that God made was very **good**.

10. God **rested** on the seventh day and made it holy.

Applying God's Word

1. People are the most important visible creatures God made. Explain. **(God created Adam and Eve in His image and gave them authority over the rest of creation. Angels are God's foremost invisible creation.)**

2. All Scripture points to God and His love for us in Christ Jesus. How does God's designation of the seventh day remind us of Jesus? See Matthew 11:28. **(God designed the seventh day to be a day of rest. Jesus invites us to find our rest in the forgiveness, new life, and salvation He has won for us.)**

3. How do the teachings of evolution compare with those of Genesis 1? **(God's Word clearly describes a six-day creation. It says God created each animal according to its kind. Nowhere does the Bible suggest that animals changed into other kinds of animals over a long period of time as the teachings of evolution suggest. Evolution holds that the earth came about by natural processes, not divine power.)**

3   Adam and Eve in Paradise
(Genesis 2)

Thinking about God's Word

1. What was the difference between the way God made people and the way He made the other creatures? **(God made people in His image.)**

2. How did God make woman? **(from Adam's rib)** Did she also have the image of God? **(Yes)**

3. What place did God prepare as a home for the first married couple? **(the Garden of Eden)**

4. God revealed His glory and majesty in His great work of creation. How did He show His power? **(He made all things by the power of His Word.)** His wisdom? **(He designed an intricate, complex creation.)** His goodness? **(He made men and women to live and work together.)**

5. What is another name for Eden? **(Paradise)**

Working with God's Word

Fill in the blanks.

1. God formed man from the **dust** of the ground.

2. God breathed into man's nostrils the **breath** of life.

3. Then man became a living **being**.

4. God planted a garden in **Eden**.

5. The tree of life stood in the **middle** of the garden.

6. God put Adam into the Garden of **Eden** to work it.

7. God said, "It is not good for the man to be **alone**."

8. God said, "I will make a **helper** suitable for him."

9. The woman was made out of one of Adam's **ribs**.

10. The man said, "She shall be called **woman**, for she was taken out of man."

True or False

1. God formed woman of the dust of the ground. T **F**

2. The Lord made every tree to bear good food. **T** F

3. God put man into the garden to take care of it. **T** F

4. There were two trees from which the man and woman should not eat. T **F**

5. Adam and Eve were holy. **T** F

Applying God's Word

1. How does God describe the relationship He designed a man and a woman to enjoy in marriage? **(God calls this relationship "one flesh.")**

2. Why does God have a right to be adored by all creatures? **(He is the maker, giver, and preserver of all.)** Why has He a right to give them commandments? **(All people belong to Him; He made us.)** Why is it their duty to obey Him only? **(He is the only God; we owe Him everything.)**

3. What actions of God, recorded in Genesis 2, evidence His love for people? **(God gave Adam and Eve to each other; He created a beautiful home for them to enjoy, complete with all they needed to live a happy, fulfilling life in close communion with their Creator.)**

4 The Fall into Sin
(Genesis 3)

Thinking about God's Word

1. How did God communicate with Adam and Eve? **(He talked directly with them.)**

2. What special command had God given them? **(not to eat from the tree in the middle of the garden)**

3. How were they to show their obedience and love toward God? **(by not eating of the fruit from the tree in the center of the garden)**

4. Did they have the ability to fulfill God's command? **(Yes)**

5. Tell how the first two people became disobedient. **(They listened to the serpent and ate the forbidden fruit.)**

6. Could Adam and Eve really hide from God? **(No)**

7. What came into the world as a result of Adam and Eve's disobedience? **(sin)**

8. Whose fault is it that we are sinners? **(Each of us is responsible for our sin. But since Adam and Eve, sin has been part of the human condition.)**

9. Name four evils that have come into the world because of sin. **(Answers will vary.)**

Working with God's Word

Answer the following questions.

1. Who tempted the woman through the serpent? **the devil**

2. Who tempted the man? **the devil, through Eve**

3. Who said they were not to eat of the tree of the knowledge of good and evil? **God**

4. Who spoke the first lie in the world? **the serpent**

5. How did the fruit look to the woman? **good for food and pleasing to the eye**

6. Why did they try to hide from God? **They were frightened of His righteous judgment.**

7. Where did they think they could hide? **among the trees of the garden**

Draw a line under the answer that makes each sentence correct.

1. A serpent is a (servant—**snake**—eel).

2. This lesson is taken from the Bible in the Book of (Exodus—Numbers—**Genesis**).

3. Crafty means (hard—brave—**sly**—wise).

4. The serpent spoke first to the (man—**woman**—snake—tree).

5. The forbidden tree was the tree of (life—**knowledge**).

6. The devil tried to make the woman (**curious**—proud—afraid).

7. (God—**Man and woman**—Animals) brought sin into the world.

Applying God's Word

1. What tactic did the devil successfully use to tempt Adam and Eve to sin? **(The devil in the form of a serpent led Adam and Eve to doubt God's words.)**

2. Explain the meaning of the phrase "The eyes of both of them were opened." **(Having fallen into sin, Adam and Eve were no longer innocent; they had fallen from a state of holiness into the sinful human condition we also know today.)**

3. Why did Adam and Eve's relationship with God change when they sinned? **(The fall into sin destroyed the image of God in Adam and Eve; they were no longer able to please God or to commune closely with Him as they had done prior to the fall.)**

5 The Promise of the Savior

(Genesis 3)

Thinking about God's Word

1. What was the complete punishment the man and the woman deserved because of their sin? **(death and eternal separation from God)**

2. What sentence did God pronounce on the woman? **(pain in childbirth; submission to her husband)** on the man? **(difficulty and frustration [the ground became cursed], death)**

3. How was the serpent punished? **(He would crawl on his belly and eat dust.)**

4. Why did God clothe Adam and Eve after they had sinned? **(God still loved them.)**

5. Why did God not let them eat of the tree of life? **(By eating of this tree they would live forever in their sin.)**

6. What is the most terrible consequence of sin? You will find the answer in Romans 6:23. **(death)**

7. How did you become a sinner? **(All people are born into sin.)**

8. What are some of the things Adam left behind when he lost Paradise? **(holiness, peace, close relationship with God and Eve)**

9. Look forward with Adam. Why could he still have hope in God's beautiful world? **(God promised the Savior; He still loved His people.)**

10. Look upward with Adam. What did he believe? What do you believe? **(He believed in the coming Savior. We believe in Jesus, the Savior who has come to defeat sin, death, and Satan for us.)**

Working with God's Word

Answer the questions with one word.

1. Whom did the Lord God call? **Adam**

2. How did Adam say he felt toward God? **afraid**

3. Whom did the man blame for his sin? **Eve**

4. Whom did the woman blame for her sin? **serpent**

5. Whom did the Lord God punish first? **serpent**

6. Who would crush the head of the devil? **Jesus**

7. Who was to bring forth children in sorrow? **Eve**

8. For whose sake was the ground cursed? **Adam's**

9. Who guarded the way to the tree of life? **cherubim**

Draw a line under the correct answer to each question.

1. Whose fault was it that Adam sinned? (devil's—Eve's—God's—**Adam's**)

2. Whose fault was it that Eve sinned? (devil's—serpent's—God's—**Eve's**)

3. Who drove Adam and his wife from the garden? (devil—cherubim—**God**—wild animals)

4. Why did Adam and his wife try to hide from God? (They were naked—They were as gods—**They had sinned**)

5. How did God punish Adam, his wife, and the serpent? (He killed them—He scolded them—**He cursed them**)

6. Who are sinners? (only heathen—all except Christians—only grown people—**all people**)

7. For whose sake did God curse the ground? (His sake—the woman's—**Adam's**—Satan's)

Applying God's Word

1. In what ways do you experience the consequences of Adam's sin in your life? **(Answers will include offenses against one or more of the Ten Commandments and the consequences these offenses have brought into the lives of the students and others.)**

2. How did Jesus, the offspring of Eve, crush the head of the serpent? **(Jesus crushed the head of the serpent when He successfully lived a perfect life and died an atoning death for the sins of all people. Jesus' words "It is finished" refer to the completion of Jesus' work and the final defeat of Satan.)**

3. What does the account teach us about God's regard for sin? **(God hates sin; those who sin cannot enjoy a close relationship with the holy and righteous God.)** for sinners? **(God still loves people in spite of their sin. He sent His only Son to pay the penalty all people deserve because of their sin.)**

6 Cain and Abel

(Genesis 4)

Thinking about God's Word

1. What is a way that Cain and Abel worshiped God? **(They brought God offerings.)**

2. How did Cain first show his anger after God did not respect his offering? **(Cain killed Abel.)**

3. Answer this question correctly for Cain and give a reason for your answer: "Am I my brother's keeper?" **(Yes, God would have us love and care for all others.)**

4. Was the mark that God set on Cain a blessing or a punishment? **(a blessing)** Why? **(God put a mark on Cain so that no one would kill him.)**

Working with God's Word

Answer each question with one word or a short phrase.

1. What name did Adam give his wife? **Eve**

2. Who was Eve's first child? **Cain**

3. Who was Eve's second child? **Abel**

4. What did Cain bring as an offering to God? **fruits of the soil**

5. What did Abel bring? **fat portions from the firstborn of his flock**

6. With whose offering was the Lord pleased? **Abel's**

7. Why was Cain cursed? **He killed his brother.**

8. What would no longer yield crops for Cain? **the ground**

9. How did the Lord protect Cain from being killed? **God put a mark on Cain so that no one would kill him.**

Draw a line under the word that makes each sentence true.

1. The name Eve means (evil—ever—**mother**—woman).

2. Killing is forbidden in the (Third—Fourth—**Fifth**—Sixth) Commandment.

3. Abel was a (farmer—carpenter—mason—**shepherd**).

4. Cain was a (**farmer**—carpenter—mason—shepherd).

5. God cursed Cain and made him a (foreigner—**wanderer**—beggar—sinner).

6. Adam was the (brother—mother—**father**—uncle) of Cain and Abel.

7. Cain (**could**—could not) have had his sin forgiven.

Applying God's Word

1. Before Cain killed Abel, Cain received a warning from God. How does God's warning apply to all people? **(God told Cain, "But if you do not do what is right, sin is crouching at your door; it desires to have you, but you must master it." All people do well to heed this same warning. Sin desires to pull us away from our Savior and to hold us firmly in its grasp so that we will not go to God to receive the forgiveness He freely offers us in Jesus.)**

2. How Did God show His love for Cain, even after Cain had sinned? **(God put a mark on Cain to protect him from those who might kill or otherwise harm him.)**

3. In what important way did God show His love for sinners such as you and me? **(God sent Jesus to take our sins upon Himself and to pay in full the penalty we deserved because of them.)**

7 From Adam to Noah
(Genesis 5)

Thinking about God's Word

1. Which words tell that Adam's children did not have the image of God as Adam had it before the fall? **(Adam had a son "in his own image.")**

2. When Adam died, which words of the Lord came true? See Lesson 5. **(Death resulted because of sin.)**

3. The time of each firstborn son is called a generation. How many generations were there from Adam to Noah? **(9; Noah is the ninth generation after Adam.)**

4. What does it mean that "men began to call on the name of the LORD"? **(Public worship began.)**

5. Which words tell us that Enoch loved God? **("Enoch walked with God.")**

Working with God's Word

Answer each question with one word or number.

1. How old was Adam when Seth was born? **130**

2. How old did Adam live to be? **930**

3. Who was Seth's first son? **Enosh**

4. Who was the oldest man who lived from Adam to Noah? **Methuselah**

5. Whom did the Lord take to heaven without letting him die? **Enoch**

6. How long did Noah's father live? **777 years**

7. How many sons did Noah have? **3**

Draw a line under the correct answer to each question.

1. What was the age of the oldest man in the world? (905—**969**—912—996)

2. Who was Adam's son? (Enosh—Jared—Methuselah—**Seth**)

3. Who went to heaven alive? (Enosh—**Enoch**—Adam—Seth)

4. How many years did Adam live after Seth was born? (600—700—**800**—900)

5. Who was Noah's son? (Enosh—Enoch—**Shem**—Lamech)

6. Why did these early Bible people get so old? (They were healthy—They had good doctors—They never worked too hard—**God wanted them to teach others**)

Applying God's Word

1. In what way do each of us still bear the image of Adam? **(Each of us is a sinner, just as our first parents, Adam and Eve, became sinners after the fall.)**

2. During whose lifetime did public worship begin? **(Public worship began during the lifetime of Seth.)** How do you suppose people worshiped God from the time of Adam to that time? **(Prior to the time when public worship began, people probably worshiped God in families, just as they do today but without the added benefit of public worship.)**

3. How did God show in the case of Enoch that He would give eternal life to those who believed in the promised Savior? **(Enoch did not die; God simply took him to heaven.)**

8 The Flood
(Genesis 6–9)

Thinking about God's Word

1. What did the Lord see when men increased in number? **(great wickedness)**

2. What did the Lord plan to do? **(wipe mankind from the face of the earth)**

3. How was Noah different from the other people? **(Noah was righteous; he walked with God.)**

4. What did God tell Noah to do? **(build an ark)**

5. How do the words "Noah did everything just as God commanded him" show that Noah believed God? **(Noah showed his obedience in the things he said and did.)**

6. Which people were saved by the ark? **(Noah, his wife, their sons and their wives, eight people in all.)**

7. Why can God not take pleasure in wickedness nor let evil dwell with Him? **(God is holy.)**

Working with God's Word

Answer each question with one word, a number, or a short phrase.

1. What happened to people as they began to increase in number? **They became very wicked.**

2. What did the Lord say He would do with people? **wipe them from the face of the earth**

3. What did the Lord tell Noah to build? **ark**

4. How many days and nights did it rain? **40**

5. How many days did the water stay on earth? **150**

6. What did Noah do after he left the ark? **He built an altar and worshiped God.**

7. What did the Lord place in the sky as a sign that He would not send another flood to destroy the whole earth? **rainbow**

Answer each question.

1. Did God send a flood to destroy the world because the people were wicked? **Yes** No

2. Did it rain for 50 days and 50 nights? Yes **No**

3. Were the mountains covered with water? Yes No *Typo*

4. Did the water remain on the earth 200 days? Yes **No**

5. Did the ark come to rest on Ararat? **Yes** No

6. Were all people and all animals destroyed by the flood? Yes **No**

7. Does God punish wickedness today? **Yes** No

Applying God's Word

1. Why was Noah declared righteous before God? See Hebrews 11:7. **(By faith Noah, warned about the coming destruction, built an ark and condemned the unrepentant world.)**

2. Which blessing that God first gave to Adam and Eve did He now give again to Noah and his family? **(God told them to be fruitful and increase in number and fill the earth.)**

3. The great flood reminds us of the Sacrament of Holy Baptism. See 1 Peter 3:18–22. Explain. **(Just as God saved Noah and his family through the waters of the flood, God saves people today through faith in the triune God by the washing of water and the Word in Holy Baptism.)**

9 The Tower of Babel
(Genesis 11)

Thinking about God's Word

1. What did people decide to do instead of spreading out over the earth? **(stay in one place to build a city and a tower that reached to the heavens)**

2. What sins did the people commit by saying the following:

   a. "Come, let us build ourselves a city"? **(The people were sinfully prideful and self-focused.)**

   b. "Let us build ourselves a tower that reaches to the heavens"? **(In their pride they sought to make a name for themselves.)**

   c. Let us "make a name for ourselves"? **(They were displacing God with their own sinful pride and ambition.)**

3. How and why did God confuse the people? **(God gave the people different languages so that they could not continue their ungodly, prideful plans.)**

4. How did the changing of languages keep the people from building their city and tower? **(People could not work together to complete their self-glorifying task because they could not communicate with one another.)**

Working with God's Word

Fill in the blanks.

1. The whole **earth** had one language.

2. The people said to each other, "Let us build ourselves a **city** with a tower."

3. They said, "Let us make a **name** for ourselves."

4. God said, "Let Us go down and confuse their **language**."

5. So the Lord **scattered** them.

Fill in the blanks with words from below.

1. These people found a **plain** where they wished to stay.

2. The **Lord** was displeased with the people.

3. The Lord punished the people by changing their **language**.

4. The Lord scattered them over the face of the **earth**.

5. The people of Babel were **proud**.

earth	language	
plain	proud	Lord

Applying God's Word

1. Which pronoun reminds us that our God is triune—three persons in one Godhead? **(God said, "Come, let Us go down and confuse their language so they will not understand each other" [Genesis 11:7].)**

2. How did the people of Babel transgress God's commandments? **(They broke the First Commandment.)** What was their punishment? **(They were given various languages and were scattered over the face of the whole earth.)**

3. Not all pride is sinful. What is wrong with the pride of the people of Babel? See 1 Corinthians 1:30–31. **(Sinful pride is that which people have in themselves and their accomplishments outside of Christ. Godly pride focuses on Christ and the blessings He provides to us through His life, death, and resurrection.)**

10 The Call of Abram
(Genesis 12)

Thinking about God's Word

1. What command came to Abram, whom God later named Abraham, from the Lord? **("Leave your country and your father's household.")**

2. Where did God want Abraham to go? **(to a land God would show him)** What did Abraham have to leave behind? **(his home and some relatives)**

3. What threefold promise did God give with His command? **(God would make Abram into a great nation and bless him; God would make his name great and make him a blessing; all people on earth would be blessed through Abram.)**

4. Which of these promises meant the same as the promise given to Adam and Eve after the fall? **(All people on earth would be blessed through Abram.)**

5. Which words show that Abraham believed God and did what He said? **("Abram left, as the Lord had told him.")**

6. How did Abraham worship God in public after he arrived in Canaan? **(He built an altar and called on God's name.)**

7. How did the Lord answer him when Abraham said that he was still childless? **(He promised him as many descendants as the stars in the sky.)**

8. Why did it take great faith on Abraham's part to believe this promise? **(He was old and still had no children.)**

9. What does it mean to have faith in God? **(To believe that God's promises are true and to trust in them even when they don't seem possible.)**

Working with God's Word

Answer each question.

1. When God called Abraham out of his homeland, which persons went with Abraham? **his wife, Sarah, and his nephew Lot**

2. Near which city did Lot pitch his tent? **Sodom**

3. How old was Abraham when God came to him another time? **99**

4. Who gave Abraham faith? **God**

5. How did God call you and give you faith? **through His Word, heard, read, or received in Baptism**

Answer each question with a word from below.

1. Who was Abraham's nephew? **Lot**

2. Which word tells that Abraham had no children? **childless**

3. Which word means family? **household**

4. Which city was filled with wicked men and sinners? **Sodom**

5. Which word tells that Abraham had faith? **believed**

household	Shem	Sodom	believed
Ur	childless	Lot	Jordan

Applying God's Word

1. In what way have all people on earth been blessed through Abraham? **(All people have been blessed through Abraham in that God sent His Son into the world to redeem the world. God's Son was a descendant of Abraham.)**

2. In addition to Abraham's actual descendants, who else is included among the children of Abraham? See Galatians 3:29. **(All who believe in Jesus as their Savior are the children of Abraham whether they are actual physical descendants or Gentile believers.)**

3. Abraham believed the Lord, and He credited it to him as righteousness. How is God's righteousness credited to people today? **(Just as with Abraham, righteousness is credited to those who believe in Jesus as the Son of God and only Savior of the world.)**

11 The Promise of Isaac
(Genesis 18)

Thinking about God's Word

1. In what form did the Lord come to Abraham at the time of this story? **(Three men came to Abraham; one was the Lord Himself.)**

2. For what special purpose had the Lord come to Abraham? **(to tell Abraham he and Sarah would have a son)**

3. How did Sarah hear the Lord's promise, even though it was not spoken directly to her? **(Sarah was listening at the entrance to the tent.)**

4. How would you answer the question "Why did Sarah laugh?" **(She laughed since she was old and well past childbearing years.)**

5. Name a promise God makes to us that has not yet been fulfilled. Do you believe it will be fulfilled? Give a reason. **(Answers may vary somewhat; students may mention Jesus' promise to come again.)**

Working with God's Word

Answer each question.

1. Who were the three men who came to Abraham's tent? **the Lord and two angels**

2. How did Abraham show kindness toward them? **He served them food.**

3. Which words show that the men accepted Abraham's invitation? **They responded, "Very well, do as you say" to Abraham's invitation.**

4. What foods did they have for their meal? **bread, curds, and a prepared calf**

5. What promise did the Lord give Abraham? **Abraham and Sarah were to have a son.**

6. How can you tell that Sarah did not believe the promise? **She laughed.**

7. Why could Sarah hardly believe that she would have a son? **She was old and past childbearing years.**

8. How did the Lord know that Sarah laughed? **The Lord knows all things.**

9. Why did Sarah deny that she had laughed? **She was afraid.**

Fill in each blank with a word from below.

1. Abraham **ran** to meet the men.

2. Sarah used flour to make **bread**.

3. A servant prepared a **calf**.

4. The Lord said, "Sarah your wife will have a **son**."

5. Sarah **laughed** to herself.

6. Sarah told a **lie**.

7. Nothing is too **hard** for the Lord.

ran	son	hard	
bread	laughed	lie	calf

Applying God's Word

1. What characteristic of God is suggested by the question "Is anything too hard for God?" **(God is omnipotent [all-powerful]. Nothing is beyond His ability to bring it to pass.)**

2. Why can we trust God to keep all of His promises? **(God is faithful. He has revealed that quality to us. Plus, He has been faithful in all He has promised to us in the past.)**

3. In this account God took on human form to visit His people. When else did God take on human form to live among His people? See Galatians 4:4. **(God sent His Son to be born of a woman so that He might become human in order to save humanity from the curse of the fall.)**

12 Sodom and Gomorrah

(Genesis 19)

Thinking about God's Word

1. Where was Lot sitting when the angels came to him? **(in the gateway of the city)**

2. Where did Lot take the angels? **(to his house)**

3. Which words show that Lot tried to turn the men of Sodom from their evil ways? **("No, my friends. Don't do this wicked thing.")**

4. What did the angels do to the wicked men? **(They struck the men with blindness.)**

5. Why had the angels come to visit Lot? **(to bring him out of the city)**

6. Whom did the angels try to save besides Lot and his wife and daughters? **(Lot's sons-in-law)** Why were they not saved? **(They refused to leave.)**

7. What was destroyed? **(Sodom and Gomorrah)** Who was destroyed? **(All who remained in these cities were destroyed.)**

8. Whom did Lot's wife disobey when she looked back? **(the angels)** How was she punished? **(She became a pillar of salt.)**

9. Why were the people of Sodom and Gomorrah destroyed? See Genesis 18:20–32 and 2 Peter 2:6. **(They were destroyed because of their great wickedness.)**

Working with God's Word

Answer each question.

1. How did Lot show kindness to the two angels? **He brought them to his house.**

2. What did the men of Sodom want with the angels? **They wanted to have sex with them.**

3. How did the angels show their mighty power? **They blinded the men.**

4. At what time of the day did Lot and his family leave the city? **early in the morning**

5. What warning did the angels give to Lot and his family? **"Don't look back!"**

6. Who looked behind her against the angels' command? **Lot's wife**

7. How was she punished? **She became a pillar of salt.**

Circle the answer that makes each sentence true.

1. (**Two**—Three—Four—Five) angels came to visit Lot.

2. The men of Sodom who came to Lot's house were (young—old—**young and old**).

3. Lot called the men of the city (sinners—**friends**—sons-in-law—heathen).

4. The two cities were burned at (**morning**—evening—noon).

5. (**Three**—Four—Five—Six) people of Sodom were saved.

Applying God's Word

1. What does this lesson teach us about God and His regard for sin? **(God is holy; He hates sin. God is also just; He punishes sin.)**

2. What evidence of God's love and mercy is contained in this account? **(God worked salvation for Lot and his two daughters.)**

3. Explain how this account prefigures the events of the Last Day. **(The destruction of Sodom and Gomorrah by fire and brimstone prefigures the Last Day, when the entire creation will be consumed by fire [2 Peter 3:10]. Only those who trust the Lord's Word will be saved.)**

13 The Offering of Isaac
(Genesis 22)

Thinking about God's Word

1. What did Abraham name his son? **(Isaac)**

2. How did God test Abraham? **(He asked him to sacrifice his son as a burnt offering.)**

3. Why must God's command have been a shock to Abraham? **(Isaac was Abraham and Sarah's only son, born to them in old age.)** What did Abraham's faith in God move him to do just the same? **(Abraham's faith moved him to obey.)**

4. In which words did the angel of the Lord tell Abraham that he had passed the test? **("Now I know that you fear God, because you have not withheld from Me your son, your only son.")**

5. What did the angel of the Lord say Abraham's blessing would be? **(He would have as many descendants as the stars, and through them all nations would be blessed.)**

6. Name three ways in which Abraham's son and God's Son were the same. **(They were sons of God's promise, they both carried wood to the sacrifice, they both went willingly to be sacrificed.)**

7. God spared Abraham's son, but what did He do with His own Son? **(He sacrificed Him for the sins of the world.)**

Working with God's Word

Answer each question.

1. Why were fire, knife, and wood taken on the journey? **These were needed for the sacrifice.**

2. How did Abraham answer Isaac's question? **He said, "God Himself will provide the lamb for the burnt offering."**

3. How did Abraham show that he really meant to carry out God's command? **He tied his son and laid him on top of the wood. Then he took the knife in hand to kill him.**

4. What did the angel of the Lord say to Abraham when they talked the second time? **"Now I know that you fear God, because you have not withheld from Me your son, your only son."**

5. How can you tell that Abraham had a strong faith? **Abraham obeyed and trusted God.**

6. How many children did God promise Abraham? **as many as the stars in the sky**

7. In whom shall all the nations of the earth be blessed? **Jesus**

Draw a circle around Yes or No.

1. Did God tell Abraham to take his son to the land of Moriah? **Yes** No

2. Did it take four days before they saw the place in the distance? Yes **No**

3. Did Isaac carry the wood up the mountain? **Yes** No

4. Did Abraham kill his son? Yes **No**

5. Is the angel of the Lord the same as Jesus? **Yes** No

6. Is a ram a male sheep? **Yes** No

7. Did Abraham love God more than he loved Isaac? **Yes** No

Applying God's Word

1. How did Abraham's answer to Isaac again prove his strong faith in God? **(He told Isaac that God would provide a lamb for the sacrifice.)** How did God fulfill what Abraham said and believed a short time later? **(He provided a ram and told Abraham to sacrifice it in place of Isaac.)** What Lamb did God Himself provide as an offering about 2,000 years later? **(His only Son, Jesus)**

2. What did Abraham believe God would do to restore Isaac if Abraham would have sacrificed him? See Hebrews 11:17–19. **(Abraham believed that God would raise Isaac from the dead.)**

3. Of what great event does Abraham's belief, referred to in item 2, remind us? **(Many years later God raised Abraham's descendant Jesus from the dead.)**

14 Isaac and His Family
(Genesis 27)

Thinking about God's Word

1. Who was Isaac's older son? **(Esau)**

2. How can you tell that Isaac intended to give the blessing to Esau? **(He told Esau he would give him the blessing.)**

3. How did Rebekah try to stop that? **(She sent Jacob, disguised as Esau, to Isaac.)**

4. How did Jacob lie to his father? **(He said, "I am Esau.")**

Working with God's Word

Answer each question.

1. How old was Isaac when he got married? **40**

2. Who were Isaac's two sons? **Esau and Jacob**

3. To whom did Isaac wish to give the blessing? **Esau**

4. How did Rebekah make Jacob's skin feel like Esau's? **She covered it with goatskins.**

5. From which animals did Rebekah make tasty food? **goats**

6. Why was it easy to fool Isaac? **Isaac could no longer see.**

7. Which blessing did Isaac give to Jacob? **the blessing of the firstborn**

On the blank lines write the word from below that answers the question.

1. What did Isaac want Esau to get for him? **food**

2. How many goats did Rebekah use to get meat ready for Isaac? **two**

3. When Jacob came into his father's room, who did he say he was? **Esau**

4. Whose voice did Isaac think he heard when Jacob was in the room? **Jacob's**

5. Whose hands did Isaac think he felt when Jacob was in the room? **Esau's**

| Esau | food | Esau's | |
| three | two | Jacob's | Abraham |

Applying God's Word

1. How did Jacob break each of the following commandments:

   a. Honor your father and your mother. **(Jacob deceived his father.)**

   b. You shall not steal. **(Jacob stole the blessing his father planned to give to Esau.)**

2. Of what was Rebekah guilty? **(Rebekah took matters into her own hands rather than trusting in God. God had promised that Jacob was to receive the greater blessing.)**

3. What does Jesus' life, death, and resurrection mean for all repentant sinners? **(Jesus has earned forgiveness for all sins ever committed, including those of Jacob and his family.)**

15 Jacob's Stairway
(Genesis 28)

Thinking about God's Word

1. Where had Esau been while Jacob was receiving the blessing from his father? **(out hunting)**

2. Which words of his blessing do you think led Esau to hate his brother and want to kill him? **(He would serve his brother.)**

3. How did God appear to Jacob after he fled? **(in a dream)**

4. In which words did the Lord give Jacob a blessing? **("I am the LORD, the God of your father Abraham and the God of Isaac. I will give you and your descendants the land on which you are lying.")**

5. What three names did Jacob give to the place where he had his dream? **(house of God, gate of heaven, and Bethel)**

6. What vow did Jacob make before he left Bethel? **("The LORD will be my God and this stone will be God's house.")**

7. Have you ever been blessed by someone? When? Where? How? Why? **(Answers will vary.)**

Working with God's Word

Answer each question.

1. What did Esau intend to do to his brother? **kill him**

2. To what place did Rebekah tell Jacob to flee? **Haran**

3. Who stood at the top of the stairway in Jacob's dream? **the Lord**

4. What name did Jacob give to the place where he dreamed? **Bethel**

5. What were the two main parts of Jacob's vow to God for His protection? **"If God will be with me and will watch over me so that I return safely to my father's house, then the LORD will be my God and this stone will be God's house."**

Answer these questions with names from below.

1. Who said, "Bless me, too, my father"? **Esau**

2. Who said, "I will give you and your descendants the land on which you are lying"? **God**

3. Who said, "You will live by the sword"? **Isaac**

4. Who said, "This is none other than the house of God"? **Jacob**

5. Who said, "This is the gate of heaven"? **Jacob**

6. Who said, "I am your son, your firstborn"? **Esau**

7. Who said, "Flee at once to my brother Laban"? **Rebekah**

God	Rebekah	Jacob
Esau	Isaac	Laban

Applying God's Word

1. Jacob received the blessing God gave to Abraham. What was the most significant part of that blessing? **(The Savior of the world would be born as a descendant.)**

2. In what ways do God's angels serve His people? **(Angels protect, serve, help, and bring messages to the people of God.)**

3. How is Bethel like a Christian church? **(A church is the house of God—the gate of heaven. A church building is set apart for the worship of God. Here God Himself is present. Jesus promises to be present wherever two or three are gathered together in His name [Matthew 18:20].)**

16 Jacob's Family
(Genesis 37)

Thinking about God's Word

1. How many wives did Jacob have? **(2)**

2. How many years did Jacob stay in Haran? **(20)** Which words show that God gave him many gifts while he was there? **(Jacob grew exceedingly prosperous.)**

3. Which words show that God wanted Jacob to return to Canaan? **("Go back to the land of your fathers and to your relatives, and I will be with you.")**

4. Why did Jacob not have to fear the long journey back to Canaan with his family? **(God promised to be with him.)**

5. Do you think Jacob made a mistake in his love for his sons? **(Answers may vary.)** Why or why not? **(Most will offer that parental preference toward children is not a good thing.)**

6. Which words tell how Joseph's brothers felt about him? **(They hated him and could not speak a kind word to him.)**

7. Which words show that the brothers and the father understood the meaning of Joseph's dreams? **(The brothers were jealous of him, but his father kept the matter in mind.)**

Working with God's Word

Answer each question.

1. For whom did Jacob serve Laban for 14 years? **(Leah and Rachel)**

2. How many years did Jacob work to earn cattle for himself? **(6)**

3. Why did Jacob return to Canaan with his family? **(The Lord told Jacob to return home.)**

4. How many sons did Jacob have? **(12)**

5. How did Jacob show his great love for Joseph? **(He made a richly ornamented robe for him.)**

6. What did the dreams mean? **(Joseph would rule over his family.)**

7. What were the names of Jacob's sons? **(Reuben, Simeon, Levi, Judah, Dan, Naphtali, Gad, Asber, Issachar, Zebulun, Joseph, and Benjamin)**

Draw a circle around Yes or No.

1. Did Joseph have 12 brothers?
   Yes   **No**

2. Did Joseph feed the flock with his brothers?
   Yes   No

3. Did Joseph make a beautiful robe?   Yes   **No**

4. Did Jacob say, "You shall indeed reign over us"?
   Yes   **No**

5. Did Jacob scold Joseph for his dreams?   **Yes**   No

Applying God's Word

1. Why do jealousy and strife exist even among the people of God? **(Jealousy and strife can be found even among God's people because believers are still sinners.)**

2. How is Jacob as a father like our Father in heaven? How is he different? **(Our heavenly Father loves us enough to provide us with the very best, just as Jacob loved Joseph and gave him a beautiful robe. Our heavenly Father loves us each with equity and to the extent that He gave His only Son to pay for our sins.)**

3. Jacob gave Joseph a beautiful robe to wear. With what are those who have been baptized in Christ clothed (Galatians 3:27)? **(By faith those who were baptized into Christ have put on Christ.)**

17 Joseph and His Brothers
(Genesis 37)

Thinking about God's Word

1. How do the words of Jacob (Israel) to Joseph show that he wanted to be a God-pleasing father? **(Israel sent Joseph to see if all was well with his brothers.)**

2. What name did the brothers call Joseph? **(dreamer)** Explain why "name-calling" is a sin against the Fifth Commandment. **(Name-calling can diminish the quality of others' lives.)**

3. What did the brothers do after they threw Joseph into a cistern? **(They sold him.)** How did this show their hard-heartedness? **(They hoped they would never see Joseph again.)**

4. How did the brothers deceive their father? **(They took Joseph's robe and dipped it in goat's blood so their father would think Joseph had been killed by a wild animal.)**

5. Show how from this lesson the brothers hurt Joseph, Jacob, and most of all themselves. Which words of Jacob tell how deeply he was hurt? **(Joseph became a slave, Jacob went into a prolonged period of mourning, and the brothers had to live with what they had done to their brother. Jacob said, "In mourning will I go down to the grave to my son.")**

Working with God's Word

Answer each question.

1. Where did Jacob's sons go to feed the flocks? **near Shechem**

2. Whom did Jacob send to see how the brothers were doing? **Joseph**

3. Who suggested that Joseph be thrown into a cistern? **Reuben**

4. Which brother suggested selling Joseph? **Judah**

5. Who bought Joseph from the brothers? **Ishmaelites**

6. How many shekels of silver were paid for Joseph? **20**

7. How did Jacob show that he believed the brother's lie? **He mourned the death of Joseph.**

Fill in the blank spaces with words from below.

1. The brothers said, "Let's **kill** him."

2. **Reuben** tried to rescue Joseph.

3. They **stripped** Joseph of his robe.

4. **Judah** said, "Come, let's sell him."

5. They sold him to the **Ishmaelites**.

6. Reuben **tore** his clothes when he saw the empty cistern.

7. Jacob said, "Some ferocious animal has **devoured** him."

Reuben	tore	stripped
Ishmaelites	Judah	kill
devoured		

Applying God's Word

1. Use this story to explain how sin sometimes escalates into other sins. **(Among Joseph's brothers jealously evoked hatred, which led to the betrayal and selling of Joseph.)**

2. Reuben pleaded with his brothers for Joseph's life. Who pleads with God on our behalf? **(Jesus pleads with His Father in heaven for us and for all for whom He has died [Romans 8:34].)**

3. How were Jesus and Joseph alike? How were they not alike? **(Joseph and Jesus were hated, betrayed, and sold by sinful companions. Jesus, however, was without sin. Joseph, like all of us, was a sinner.)**

18 Joseph Serves Pharaoh
(Genesis 41)

Thinking about God's Word

1. Why did Pharaoh have to find someone in place of his magicians to interpret his dreams? **(They could not interpret them.)**

2. How did Pharaoh know that Joseph could interpret dreams? (See Genesis 41:9–13.) **(The chief cupbearer told him.)**

3. How did Joseph show his humility as he stood before Pharaoh? **(He told Pharaoh that he could not interpret dreams, but that God would reveal the meaning of the dreams to him.)**

4. In which words did Joseph give all honor and glory to God? **("God will give Pharaoh the answer he desires.")**

5. What advice did Joseph give Pharaoh together with the interpretation? **(Joseph told Pharaoh to put a wise and discerning man in charge of the land of Egypt and to take a fifth of the harvest during the seven years of abundance as a reserve for the seven years of famine.)**

Working with God's Word

Answer each question with one word or a short phrase.

1. Who had dreams in this lesson? **Pharaoh**

2. How many cows did Pharaoh see coming from the water? **7**

3. What kind of grain grew on the stalks Pharaoh saw in his dream? **healthy and good**

4. Whom did Pharaoh first ask to interpret his dreams? **magicians**

5. According to Joseph, who alone could answer Pharaoh's dreams? **God**

6. How many years of plenty and famine would there be? **7 each**

7. Whom did Pharaoh choose as one discerning and wise? **Joseph**

8. Throughout which land did Joseph travel? **Egypt**

9. What did he collect? **one-fifth of the grain**

Underline the word that makes each sentence true.

1. Pharaoh was the (**king**—captain—president—prince) of Egypt.

2. Pharaoh's dreams told about (14—**7**—10—16) years of famine.

3. Joseph said that (he—magicians—Jacob—**God**) would answer Pharaoh.

4. Pharaoh put Joseph in charge of (**Egypt**—Israel—food—people).

5. Joseph gathered (**one-fifth**—one-half—all—one-sixth) of the crops during the seven years of plenty.

Applying God's Word

1. How did Joseph rise from slave and prisoner to ruler of Egypt? **(God blessed Joseph with discernment and wisdom.)**

2. What words of Joseph indicate his faith in God? **(Joseph told Pharaoh, "God will give Pharaoh the answer he desires.")**

3. What did Pharaoh recognize about Joseph that made Joseph an ideal candidate for a position of authority in Egypt? **(Pharaoh said, "Since God has made all this known to you, there is no one so discerning and wise as you.")**

The Journeys of Joseph's Brothers
(Genesis 42–43)

Thinking about God's Word

1. How can you tell that there was a famine also in Canaan during the lean years? **(Jacob sent his sons to Egypt to buy food.)**

2. What news had Jacob received from Egypt? **(He heard there was food in Egypt.)**

3. How did Joseph treat the brothers when they came to him? **(He was harsh and stern with them.)**

4. According to the words of Jacob, who alone could grant mercy? **(God Almighty)**

5. Why did Joseph weep? **(He recognized his brothers.)**

6. How can you tell that Joseph still remembered all of his brothers? **(Joseph had his brothers seated according to their age.)**

7. Why do you suppose Joseph gave Benjamin a greater portion of goods than the others? **(Benjamin was his youngest brother, Jacob's other son by Rachel.)**

Working with God's Word

Answer each question.

1. Where was there plenty of grain? **Egypt**

2. Why did Jacob need grain from Egypt? **The famine was severe in the land.**

3. Whom did Jacob send to get the grain? **his sons**

4. Which brother did Joseph want to see? **Benjamin**

5. Whom did Joseph order bound? **Simeon**

6. Why did the father not want Benjamin to go to Egypt? **Benjamin was the youngest son, Jacob's only remaining child by Rachel.**

7. What would happen to Jacob if something happened to Benjamin? **He would die in sorrow.**

Fill in the blank spaces with words from below.

1. Ten of Joseph's **brothers** went to buy grain.

2. They **bowed** down to Joseph.

3. Joseph turned away from them and began to **weep**.

4. Joseph gave orders to get **grain** for his brothers.

5. Joseph's brothers **ate** with him.

ate	brothers	bowed
grain	weep	true	guilty

Answer each question with one word or a phrase.

1. Where did Jacob ask his sons to go again a second time? **Egypt**

2. When did Joseph want his brothers to eat with him? **at noon**

3. How did Joseph show that he loved Benjamin? **He gave him five times more food than the others.**

4. Who got five measures of food? **Benjamin**

5. What did Joseph command to be put into Benjamin's sack beside the grain? **his silver cup**

Circle Yes or No.

1. Did Jacob say, "I have heard that there is grain in Egypt"? **Yes** No

2. Did Joseph's brothers recognize him? Yes **No**

3. Were Joseph's brothers invited for supper? Yes **No**

4. Was Jacob still alive at this time? **Yes** No

5. Did Benjamin get four times as much as his brothers? Yes **No**

Applying God's Word

1. How could Joseph easily have taken revenge on his brothers for having sold him? **(Joseph was now a mighty ruler in Egypt. He literally had the lives of his brothers in his hand.)** Why didn't he? **(Joseph believed in God and sought to do God's will.)**

2. How does Judah's regard for his brother remind you of Jesus' love for you? **(Judah offered himself in protection of his brother Benjamin. Jesus offered Himself for us and for our salvation.)**

3. God knows each of us even better than Joseph knew his brothers. Explain. See also Matthew 10:30. **(God knows us intimately; He made us. He even knows the number of hairs on our heads.)**

20 Joseph Makes Himself Known to His Brothers
(Genesis 44–45)

Thinking about God's Word

1. Of what did the steward accuse the brothers? **(stealing)**

2. How can you tell from the answer of the brothers that they were sure none of them had done the wrong? **(They said that if any of them had the cup he would die, and the rest would become Joseph's slaves.)**

3. Why did the brothers all return to the city when the guilty one was found? **(They knew they had to return to Jacob with Benjamin.)**

4. Whom only did Joseph say he wanted to keep as a servant? **(Benjamin)** Why? **(Joseph wanted to see whether his brothers had changed.)**

5. How did the words of Judah show that his heart was changed? **(Judah offered to serve as a slave in Benjamin's place.)**

6. How can you tell that this is what Joseph had hoped for in testing his brothers? **(Joseph wept, asked about their father, and told them who he was.)**

7. Why were the brothers afraid at first? **(They feared Joseph would seek revenge on them.)**

Working with God's Word

Answer each question.

1. What did Joseph command his steward to do? **to go after his brothers**

2. How did the brothers show sorrow and repentance? **They offered to do whatever they could to save Benjamin.**

3. How did Judah keep his promise to Jacob? **He promised to serve as a slave in Benjamin's place.**

4. What did Joseph tell the brothers after he heard Judah? **"I am Joseph."**

5. Why were the brothers afraid of Joseph? **They feared his retribution.**

6. What did Joseph say to prove that he still trusted God? **He said God had sent him ahead to save lives.**

7. How did Joseph want to take care of his father and brothers? **He wanted to provide for them in Egypt.**

Draw a line under the correct answer to each question.

1. Who had taken the cup from Joseph? (Benjamin—Judah—Reuben—**no one**)

2. Who wanted to take Benjamin's place and become a slave? (Reuben—Simeon—**Judah**)

3. What did Judah call Joseph? (king—brother—**lord**—ruler)

4. Whom did Joseph kiss? (only Benjamin—only Reuben—only Simeon—**all the brothers**)

5. How did Joseph show that he was a true child of God? (He wept—He nourished—**He forgave**—He supplied)

6. Which of the brothers was dearest to Joseph's heart? (**Benjamin**—Reuben—Judah—Simeon)

7. How did Joseph reward evil? (with evil—**with good**)

Applying God's Word

1. What did Joseph say and do to show his brothers that he forgave them? **(Joseph told his brothers he would provide for them in Egypt; he wept and kissed them.)**

2. Which words show that Joseph honored God as much now as he did when he was in trouble? **(Joseph credited God for making him lord of all Egypt.)**

3. Why did Joseph forgive his brothers? Read Colossians 3:13. **(Joseph forgave, just as God had forgiven him.)**

21 Jacob and Joseph Are Reunited

(Genesis 46–50)

Thinking about God's Word

1. Why did Joseph send carts to Canaan? **(to bring his family to Egypt)**

2. In his parting words to his brothers, how did Joseph show that he was a good brother? **(He told them not to quarrel along the way.)**

3. What did Jacob say when he was finally convinced that Joseph was alive? **("I'm convinced! My son Joseph is still alive. I will go and see him before I die.")**

4. How can you tell that Jacob was happy and at peace after he saw Joseph? **(It says that his spirit revived.)**

5. Why did the brothers ask Joseph to forgive their trespasses again after their father died? **(They feared Joseph would hurt them after their father had died.)** What was Joseph's answer? **(He assured them of his love and forgiveness.)**

Working with God's Word

Answer each question with one word or a phrase.

1. How many shekels of silver did Joseph give to Benjamin? **300**

2. To whom did the brothers bring the good news? **Jacob**

3. Whom did Jacob send before him to meet Joseph? **Judah**

4. What kind of cart did Joseph use to meet his father? **chariot**

5. Who was afraid after Jacob died? **Joseph's brothers**

6. What did they ask of Joseph? **"Forgive your brothers the sins and wrongs they committed in treating you so badly."**

7. Who intended everything for good? **God**

Fill in the blank spaces with words from below.

1. Joseph gave each brother new **clothes**.

2. The silver and clothing were signs of Joseph's **love**.

3. When Jacob saw Joseph again, he was ready to **die**.

4. Joseph went to meet his father in a **chariot**.

5. Joseph settled his **father** and brothers in Egypt.

6. Jacob called his sons and **blessed** them before he died.

7. After Jacob had died, the brothers sent word to Joseph and asked him to **forgive** them.

clothes	forgive	die	
father	love	Judah	
hate	blessed	chariot	multiplied

Applying God's Word

1. Why was it better for Jacob to go to Egypt to live with Joseph than for Joseph to go to Canaan to live with Jacob? **(Joseph was ruler in Egypt, where there was food.)**

2. How did Joseph's answer and his action again show his faith in God and his love for the brothers? **(Joseph recognized God at work throughout his life.)**

3. Read Romans 8:28. What things seemed evil in Joseph's life? **(He was betrayed by his family and associates numerous times.)** How did God work for good in all things? **(Through all that happened, God placed Joseph in a position to save his family.)**

22 The Birth of Moses
(Exodus 1–2)

Thinking about God's Word

1. How did the Lord bless the family of Israel in Egypt? **(They grew to a large number.)** Why didn't the new pharaoh like this? **(He feared their strength.)** How did he try to "deal shrewdly with them"? **(He made them slaves and made a law stating that all male babies born to them should be thrown into the Nile.)**

2. How do you explain the fact that "the more they were oppressed, the more they multiplied"? **(In the midst of their trouble, God still blessed them.)** Of which blessing of God to Abraham are you reminded? **(That Abraham's descendants would be as numerous as the stars in the sky.)**

3. Why did Pharaoh want the baby boys drowned? **(to diminish the number and strength of the people)**

4. Think of two good reasons why the Levite woman did not drown her son. **(She obeyed God; she loved her son.)** Why did she not keep him at home longer? **(She was unable to hide him anymore.)** Why did she place him by the river? **(Perhaps she saw this action as one way to obey Pharaoh's command. Perhaps she hoped Pharaoh's daughter would find him and have pity on him.)**

5. Was it merely by chance that the baby's sister was there when the princess came to bathe? **(No)** How were the mother and daughter wise? **(The mother saw an opportunity for the baby to be saved. The daughter saw an opportunity for the baby to be returned to his mother.)** What did God have to do with their wisdom? **(God blessed it.)**

6. Why did the princess keep the baby she had found? **(He was crying and she felt sorry for him.)**

7. Who gave Moses his name? **(Pharaoh's daughter)** Exodus 2:10 will tell you what it means. **(She named him Moses, saying, "I drew him out of the water.")**

Working with God's Word

Answer each question.

1. Whom did the king not know about? **Joseph**

2. How did the king hope to crush the Israelites? **He made them slaves.**

3. What very cruel law did he make? **Every boy baby was to be thrown into the Nile.**

4. Which mother did not obey this law? **Moses' mother**

5. What did she make in which to hide her son? **a papyrus basket**

6. What did the mother do with the baby after three months? **placed him on the banks of the Nile**

7. Who came to the river to bathe? **Pharaoh's daughter**

8. Whom did the baby's sister call as nurse? **Moses' mother**

9. Why did Moses have to flee from Pharaoh? **He killed an Egyptian.**

Fill in the blanks with the words from the following page.

1. A **Levite** woman had a baby boy.

2. Pharaoh ordered, "Every **Hebrew boy** that is born you must throw into the Nile."

3. Moses' mother made him a basket out of **papyrus.**

4. The baby's **sister** stood at a distance and watched.

5. Pharaoh's daughter saw a **basket** among the reeds.

6. The baby's sister asked, "Shall I go and get one of the Hebrew women to **nurse** the baby for you?"

7. And the **girl** went and got the baby's mother.

8. Moses saw an **Egyptian** beating a Hebrew.

   basket
   girl
   Levite
   papyrus
   Egyptian
   sister
   nurse
   Moses
   Hebrew boy

Applying God's Word

1. Who became Moses' grandfather by adoption?
   (Pharaoh) How did it benefit Moses to live in
   the palace of the king rather than to live at home
   with his family? **(He had access to the knowledge and privileges of a prince of Egypt.)**
   How could it have been harmful? **(He might
   have been corrupted by the evil influence of
   the pagan court.)**

2. What evidence does this story provide to indicate
   that Moses identified himself with the people of
   God rather than with the Egyptians? **(Moses
   defended the rights of the Hebrew who was
   being beaten by the Egyptian.)**

3. Compare Jesus' birth and the birth of Moses.
   **(Both were born to people in bondage;
   Moses' parents were slaves in Egypt, and
   Jesus' mother shared humanity's bondage to
   sin. Both births were accompanied by the
   slaughter of children. Other comparisons
   may be offered.)**

23 The Call of Moses

(Exodus 3–4)

Thinking about God's Word

1. How did the Lord appear to Moses? **(The angel of the Lord appeared to Moses in a burning bush.)**

2. Why did the Lord call the Hebrews "My people"? **(They are the chosen people, the descendants of Abraham, Isaac, and Jacob.)** Why did the Lord want to help His people? **(God had promised to bless them and give them the Promised Land.)**

3. Which words show that Moses did not think himself great enough to lead God's people out of Egypt? **("Who am I, that I should go to Pharaoh and bring the Israelites out of Egypt?")**

4. How did God tell Moses that He would help him? **(God gave Moses three signs to perform.)**

5. What was Moses' second excuse? **(Moses said he was slow of speech and tongue.)**

6. What power did God give Moses to overcome that excuse? **(God said, "I will help you speak and will teach you what to say.")**

7. How did the Lord patiently answer the third excuse of Moses? **(God gave Moses his brother Aaron to speak for him.)**

Working with God's Word

Answer each question with one word or a short phrase.

1. To which mountain did Moses come? **Horeb**

2. Where did the angel of the Lord appear to Moses? **in a burning bush**

3. Where were the Lord's people? i**n slavery in Egypt**

4. To whom did God wish to send Moses? **Pharaoh**

5. Who said He would be with Moses? **God**

6. What did Moses' staff turn into? **a snake**

7. Where did Moses put his hand? **into his cloak**

8. What would become of the water poured on dry ground? **It would become blood.**

9. Who would speak for Moses? **Aaron**

Draw a circle around the word or phrase that answers each question.

1. Where were the Lord's people in misery? (**Egypt**—Canaan—Midian—Sinai)

2. How many excuses did Moses make to God? (1—2—**3**—4)

3. What turned into a snake? (Moses' hand—**Moses' staff**—Moses' shoes—Moses' sheep)

4. Where did the Lord tell Moses to put his hand? (in his pocket—over his heart—**inside his coat**—on the rod)

5. What disease came over Moses' hand? (**leprosy**—rheumatism—measles—palsy)

6. From where should Moses take water in Egypt? (**river**—well—lake—fountain)

7. Who could speak well? (**Aaron**—Moses—a priest—Pharaoh)

Applying God's Word

1. Why did the Lord become angry? **(Moses was reluctant to accept God's call.)**

2. How did living in the palace of Pharaoh prepare Moses for this work? **(Moses learned the ways of the Egyptian court and of leadership and diplomacy.)**

3. Who are the leaders of God's people today? **(pastors, teachers, and other church workers, including lay leaders)** What do we believe about their work? **(We believe that God has called them to this work.)**

24 The Passover
(Exodus 11–12)

Thinking about God's Word

1. How did Moses and Aaron tell Pharaoh that they were sent by God? **(They told Pharaoh God had said "Let My people go.")**

2. Whom did Pharaoh consider greater than the Lord? **(himself)**

3. Why didn't the miracles have any effect on Pharaoh's heart? **(The Lord had hardened Pharaoh's heart.)**

4. List all the directions the Lord told Moses to give His people about the Passover. **(Take a lamb without defect, one for each household. Slaughter it at twilight. Put some of the blood on the top and sides of the doorframes of the houses. Eat the lamb roasted over the fire along with bitter herbs and bread made without yeast. Do not leave any until morning. Eat it with your cloak tucked into your belt, your sandals on your feet, and your staff in your hand.)**

5. What would keep death from coming over the firstborn of the children of Israel? **(The lamb's blood on the doorframe of their houses)**

Working with God's Word

Fill in the blanks.

1. Moses and **Aaron** talked to Pharaoh.

2. Pharaoh asked, "Who is the **Lord**, that I should obey Him?"

3. The Lord had brought nine **plagues** upon Egypt.

4. The Lord said, "Take a lamb without **defect**."

5. "And slaughter it at **twilight**."

6. "The blood will be a **sign** for you on the houses."

7. "This is a day you are to **commemorate**."

8. The Israelites **did** just what the Lord commanded.

Draw a line under the word or phrase that makes each sentence true.

1. (Moses—Aaron—Israel—**God**) hardened Pharaoh's heart.

2. The children of Israel were to put blood on the (windows—doors—**doorframes**—steps) of their homes.

3. The children of Israel were commanded to eat (the best parts—**all**—as much as they cared for—most) of the Passover lamb.

4. God was going to pass through Egypt (**at night**—in the morning—in the afternoon—at noon).

5. The Lord was going to strike down all the (**firstborn**—youngest—girls—boys) in Egypt.

Applying God's Word

1. How were the children of Israel to remember this day in future generations? **(They were to continue their meal as a celebration commemorating the event.)** What was the feast called? **(Passover)**

2. How did the children of Israel show that they believed the Lord? **(They did what the Lord commanded.)**

3. Who is our Passover lamb? **(Jesus)** How did He become a Passover lamb for us? See 1 Corinthians 5:7. **(He shed His blood for us on the cross.)**

25 The Departure from Egypt
(Exodus 12–14)

Thinking about God's Word

1. Why was there loud wailing in Egypt? **(The Lord struck down all the firstborn in Egypt.)**

2. When did Pharaoh call Moses and Aaron? **(during the night)** Why did the Egyptians now want the Israelites to leave quickly? **(They thought that otherwise they would all die.)**

3. Why did Pharaoh want the Israelites back? **(He realized he was suddenly without a valuable labor force.)**

4. What did Moses say to the people? **("Do not be afraid. Stand firm and you will see the deliverance the LORD will bring you today. The Egyptians you see today you will never see again. The LORD will fight for you; you need only be still.")**

5. What miracle did God perform through Moses to enable the people to cross the Red Sea? **(The waters divided, and the people went through the sea on dry land.)**

6. What do you suppose the Egyptians thought when they rushed into the Red Sea after the children of Israel? **(They could pass through the same way.)** How did the Lord finally punish proud Pharaoh and his army in which he trusted? **(The waters covered them, and they drowned.)**

7. How did the Israelites thank God for His wonderful deliverance? See Exodus 15:1–21. **(They sang to the Lord.)**

Working with God's Word

Answer each question.

1. At what time did the Lord strike down all the firstborn of Egypt? **midnight**

2. In how many homes was at least one person dead? **all Egyptian houses**

3. What did Pharaoh say to Moses and Aaron now? **"Up! Leave my people! For otherwise we will all die!"**

4. How many men left Egypt? **about 600,000**

5. How did the Lord protect His people by day and by night? **He went ahead of them in a pillar of cloud by day and in a pillar of fire by night.**

6. Where did Pharaoh's army overtake the children of Israel? **as they camped by the sea**

7. What happened to Pharaoh and his men? **They drowned.**

Draw a circle around Yes or No.

1. Did the angel of Death go through Egypt at noon?   Yes **No**

2. Was Pharaoh a firstborn?   Yes **No**

3. Was a person dead in every Egyptian house? **Yes** No

4. Did the children of Israel travel on foot? **Yes** No

5. Did the children of Israel have strong faith? Yes **No**

6. Was there a wall of water on both sides of Israel? **Yes** No

7. Did Pharaoh swim to shore?   Yes **No**

Applying God's Word

1. God came to His people Israel in a pillar of cloud and in a pillar of fire. How does God come to His people today? **(God comes to His people today through the means of grace—the Word and the Sacraments.)**

2. God rescued His people from captivity in Egypt. From what forms of captivity has God rescued us? **(God has rescued us from sin, death, and the power of the devil.)**

3. How and when did His rescue of us take place? **(Jesus rescued us through His death on Calvary's cross to pay the penalty we deserved because of our sins.)**

26   The Giving of the Law

(Exodus 15–16; 19–20)

Thinking about God's Word

1. Why did the Israelites grumble? **(They had no food.)**

2. How did the Lord promise to feed them? **(He said He would send meat that night and bread in the morning.)** How did He keep His promise? **(Quail covered the camp that night, and flakes like frost appeared on the ground the next morning.)**

3. How did Moses tell the people to prepare themselves to meet with God? **(They were to wash their clothes.)**

4. With what signs did God show the people that He had something very serious and important to tell them? **(thunder, lightning and trumpet blasts, smoke and fire)**

5. Why were the people afraid? **(What they saw and heard frightened them.)** What did they say? **("Speak to us yourself and we will listen. But do not have God speak to us or we will die.")**

6. Where did God take Moses to have him receive the Law? **(Mount Sinai)**

7. What are the Ten Commandments? **(a statement of God's will for His people originally spoken by God to the people at Sinai and written on two tablets of stone called the tablets of the Testimony; see Exodus 24 and 34)**

Working with God's Word

Answer each question with a word or a short phrase.

1. Who led Israel from the Red Sea? **Moses**

2. Where did the children of Israel go after they left the Red Sea? **into the Desert of Shur**

3. Who murmured against Moses and Aaron? **the whole community**

4. What did the Lord promise Israel for twilight food? **meat**

5. Which bird did the Lord send for meat? **quail**

6. What did Israelites call the morning food? **manna**

7. How long did the children of Israel eat manna? **40 years**

8. Where did Israel camp in the third month? **in the Desert of Sinai in front of the mountain**

9. What was inscribed by the finger of God? **the two tablets of the Testimony**

Draw a line under the word that makes each sentence true.

1. Moses led Israel from the (Dead—**Red**—Caspian—Black) Sea.

2. The children of Israel went into the (forest—**desert**—water).

3. The Israelites said they were (**hungry**—thirsty—tired—weak).

4. In the (first—second—**third**—fourth) month the Israelites came to the Desert of Sinai.

5. God wanted the people to meet Him on the (first—second—**third**—fourth) day.

6. Moses was on the mountain (30—**40**—4—50) days and nights.

7. The Ten Commandments are written in Exodus, chapter (10—**20**—30—40).

Applying God's Word

1. God gave His people Israel special food. What special food has God given us? **(God in Christ has given us His very body and blood together with bread and wine for the forgiveness of sins, new life, and salvation.)**

2. What does God's Law tell us? **(God tells us God's will for our lives. It tells us what we are to do, what not to do, and how to live.)**

3. How did Jesus fulfill God's Law for us? **(Jesus kept God's Law perfectly in our place.)**

27 The Golden Calf
(Exodus 32; 34)

Thinking about God's Word

1. Why did the children of Israel become impatient with Moses? **(He was so long in coming down from the mountain.)**

2. How did the people worship the idol that Aaron had made? **(They regarded the calf as one of the gods that brought them out of Egypt.)** Why was that a sin? **(They sinned by displacing the true God with another.)**

3. What did God say to Moses when He saw the people sin? **("Go down, because your people have become corrupt; they are a stiff-necked people.")** What had God always called these people before? **("My people")**

4. What did Moses carry with him on the way down from the mount? **(two tablets bearing the Ten Commandments)** Whose writing were they? **(God's)**

5. When did Moses get angry? **(when he approached the camp and saw the calf and the people dancing)** How did he show his anger? **(He threw the tablets, breaking them.)** What did he make the people do with the idol? **(drink it after he had burned it and ground it to powder)**

6. With which words did Moses call the people to repentance? **("You have committed a great sin. But now I will go up to the LORD; perhaps I can make atonement for your sin.")**

7. How did Moses again get two tablets of stone with the Ten Commandments written on them? **(He chiseled out two stone tablets like the first ones and took them with him up the mount to get the commandments a second time.)**

Working with God's Word

Answer each question.

1. Whom did the people ask to make gods for them? **Aaron**

2. What metal did Aaron use to make the image? **gold**

3. What kind of people did God say the Israelites were? **stiff-necked**

4. Who made the first two tablets of stone? **God**

5. Who wrote the commandments on the second two tablets of stone? **God**

Fill in the blanks with words from below.

1. **Aaron** asked the people to bring their earrings.

2. The people made **burnt** offerings to the golden idol.

3. When Moses saw the dancing and the calf, he became **angry**.

4. The **Lord** wrote the Ten Commandments.

5. The people sinned against the **First** Commandment.

Lord	burnt	Sinai	
Aaron	First	angry	Levi

Applying God's Word

1. How does this account illustrate the saying "Idle hands are the devil's workshop"? **(While God's people waited for Moses, they fell into the kinds of sinful activities practiced by the pagan inhabitants of the desert through which they were traveling.)**

2. What forms of idolatry find their way into our lives today? **(People often place friends, money, power, prestige, and possessions above God.)**

3. Moses pleaded with God to forgive the people of their sins. Who pleads with God on our behalf? **(Jesus speaks to His heavenly Father in our defense [1 John 2:1].)**

28 The Bronze Snake
(Numbers 13–14; 21)

Thinking about God's Word

1. Why did God command Moses to send men into the land before the children of Israel went in? **(to explore the land)**

2. When they returned, what did the explorers report to Moses? **(The land flows with milk and honey.)** Why didn't they think the new land could be taken? **(Powerful people lived there.)**

3. What did the Israelites say? **("If only we had died in Egypt! Or in this desert! We should choose a leader and go back to Egypt.")** How did they again show their lack of trust in God? **(They grumbled.)**

4. Who did not agree with the other explorers? **(Joshua and Caleb)** In whom did they trust? **(the Lord)**

5. How long did the Lord say the Israelites would wander? **(40 years)**

6. How many Israelites did the Lord want to bring into the land of Canaan? **(all of them)** Why didn't all of them get there? **(As a consequence of their sin of grumbling against God, they were not permitted to enter the Promised Land.)**

7. How was the serpent a type of Christ? Think of these things: lowly, despised, set upon a pole, lifted up, looked upon, lived. **(Those who trusted God's promise and looked to it lived.)**

Working with God's Word

Answer each question with one word.

1. Which desert did the children of Israel leave? **Sinai**

2. Which land did the Lord want the men to search? **Canaan**

3. How did the explorers describe the people of the land? **powerful**

4. Where did the children of Israel wish they had died? **Egypt**

5. What did the people want to use to kill the two God-fearing explorers? **stones**

6. What did the Lord send among the people to punish them? **snakes**

7. Who prayed for the people? **Moses**

Draw a line under the word or phrase that answers the questions.

1. After how many days did the explorers return from Canaan? (20—30—**40**—50)

2. Which words show that the land was a good land? (grasshoppers—**milk and honey**—fruit trees—grapes)

3. Who of the older Israelites would get into Canaan? (Moses—Miriam—**Joshua**—Aaron)

4. Who sent venomous snakes among the people? (**God**—Moses—Joshua—Caleb)

5. Of what was the serpent made that Moses set upon a pole? (iron—tin—clay—**bronze**)

6. Through what did God save the people who were dying from snakebites? (**bronze snake**—Moses' staff—the cross—medicine)

Applying God's Word

1. Describe Joshua and Caleb in the face of what many would consider an overwhelming obstacle. **(Joshua and Caleb express their trust and confidence in God's ability to bring them victory over the mighty inhabitants of the land He has promised to give them.)**

2. The serpent on the pole brought restored healing to all who gazed upon it. What did Jesus bring when He was lifted up on the cross? See John 3:14–15. **(Jesus endured the cross so "that everyone who believes in Him may have eternal life.")**

3. How would the 40 years in the wilderness remind the people of their sin? What knowledge of God's grace did the people possess during their 40 years of wandering? **(The 40 years in the wilderness would remind the people of the 40 days the spies spent in the Promised Land. During their sojourn in the wilderness the people of God could be confident that, together with Joshua and Caleb, the younger generation would enter Canaan.)**

29 Israel Enters Canaan

(Deuteronomy 34; Joshua 1–5)

Thinking about God's Word

1. Just as Israel was about to enter Canaan, what did the Lord show Moses from Mount Nebo? **(the whole land)** What happened to Moses then? **(He died.)** Why does no one know where the grave of Moses is? **(People might honor Moses as God.)**

2. Why did the Lord not permit His servant Moses to go into the Promised Land? See Numbers 20:7–12. **(Moses disobeyed by striking a rock rather than speaking to it.)**

3. List the directions God gave the new leader. **("Cross the Jordan River into the land I am about to give to the Israelites. Be strong and very courageous. Do not let this Book of the Law depart from your mouth; meditate on it day and night.")** How would he be successful? **(by God's power and with His encouragement)**

4. When the people were ready to enter the land, who went first? **(the priests)** Why was this proper? **(They were carrying the ark of the covenant.)**

5. How was it possible for the Israelites to pass over the Jordan on dry ground? **(God caused the waters to part.)**

6. When did the waters of the Jordan flow as before? **(when the priests left the river)**

7. Why did the manna now stop falling from heaven? **(The people could now eat the produce of Canaan.)**

Working with God's Word

Fill in the blanks.

1. The Israelites grieved for Moses **30** days.

2. God told Joshua, "Do not let this Book of the **Law** depart from your mouth."

3. The priests carried the **ark of the covenant.**

4. The water flowing down to the **Salt** Sea was cut off.

5. Upon entering the Promised Land the people ate some unleavened bread and **roasted grain.**

Draw a line under the word or phrase that makes each sentence true.

1. (Joshua—The children of Israel—**The Lord**—Aaron) buried Moses.

2. (Caleb—Aaron—**Joshua**—Moses) was chosen by God to lead the children of Israel into Canaan.

3. Joshua said, "(**Three**—Four—Five—Six) days from now you will cross the Jordan."

4. The Israelites had to cross the (Salt Sea—**Jordan**—Red Sea—Nile) to get into the Promised Land.

Applying God's Word

1. Through what means did God promise to make Joshua prosperous and successful? **(God directed Joshua to the regular use of His Word [the Book of the Law].)**

2. God told Joshua that He would remain with him wherever he would go. How did God dramatically show His presence? **(God parted the waters of the Jordan River so that His people could enter the Promised Land on dry ground.)**

3. What are some promises God has made to you? How can you be sure that God will keep them? **(Answers will vary. We know God will keep His promises to us because He has kept every promise in the past.)**

30 The Conquest of Canaan
(Joshua 6–10)

Thinking about God's Word

1. How did the children of Israel show their faith in God's plan to take Jericho? **(They obeyed God, following His plan to capture the city.)**

2. What happened to Jericho? **(The walls fell, and the city was taken.)**

3. By what miracle did the Lord make a complete victory possible? **(He caused the walls of the city to fall down.)**

Working with God's Word

Answer the questions.

1. How many days were the armed men to go around the city one time? **6**

2. When were the armed men of war to circle the city seven times? **on the seventh day**

3. What noise did the people make on the seventh day? **They shouted.**

4. Why was it easy for the Israelites to go into the city? **The walls fell.**

5. Why did Joshua not have to fear the five kings of the Amorites? **The Lord threw them into confusion, hurling large hailstones at their army.**

Answer each question with Yes or No.

1. Did the Israelites walk around Jericho 13 times? **Yes** No

2. Did the armed men blow their trumpets? Yes **No**

3. Did it take two weeks to capture Jericho? Yes **No**

4. Did five kings of the Amorites join forces against Israel? **Yes** No

5. Did Joshua say, "O sun, stand still"? **Yes** No

6. Did the Lord give Israel the land of their forefathers? **Yes** No

7. Was Joshua the leader of Israel? **Yes** No

Applying God's Word

1. In what three ways did God act to give His people victory? **(He caused the walls of Jericho to fall down, hurled down large hailstones, and made the sun and moon to remain stationary in the sky.)**

2. What "walls" has God broken down for you? **(Answers may vary somewhat. For all of us, Jesus has destroyed the wall separating us from our heavenly Father. He has also destroyed walls of hostility and prejudice, uniting those who love and trust in Jesus.)**

3. How can you tell that the Lord provided Israel with everything they needed in the Promised Land? **(The people fought for possession of the land and no longer grumbled.)** Which promise of God to Abraham was now completely fulfilled? **(the promise of the homeland)** Which greater promise was not yet fulfilled? **(the promise of the Savior)**

31 Gideon
(Judges 6)

Thinking about God's Word

1. After the Lord had mercifully brought the children of Israel back to Canaan, what did they do? **(They did evil in the eyes of the Lord.)**

2. How did the Lord punish them? **(God gave them into the hands of the Midianites.)**

3. How did the Midianites hurt Israel? **(They camped on the land and ruined the crops.)**

4. How did Israel show that they were sorry for what they had done? **(They cried out to the Lord for help.)**

5. What did the Lord want Gideon to do? **(reduce the size of Israel's army)**

6. Why did the Lord want the army of Israel reduced to 300? **(Israel might credit themselves with the victory if they advanced with a large, powerful army.)**

7. In the words of their battle cry, how did Gideon's men show that they believed God would help them? **(They shouted, "A sword for the LORD and for Gideon!")**

Working with God's Word

Answer each question with one word or a short phrase.

1. What did the children of Israel do in the eyes of the Lord? **evil**

2. Into whose hands did the Lord deliver Israel? **Midianites**

3. Where was Gideon threshing wheat? **at a winepress**

4. Who appeared to Gideon? **the angel of the Lord**

5. Whom did Gideon send to gather the people? **messengers**

6. How many were afraid to fight? **22,000**

7. How many men did the Lord use to save Israel? **300**

8. How many men were in each company? **100**

9. Who won the battle? **God won the battle for Israel.**

Draw a line under the word or phrase that answers each question.

1. Into whose hands did the Lord give Israel? (Philistines—Amorites—Ammonites—**Midianites**)

2. What was Gideon doing at the winepress? (making wine—pressing grapes —herding sheep—**threshing wheat**)

3. How many Israelites were afraid to fight? (**22,000**—300—32,000—10,000)

4. How many were used by God to defeat the Midianites? (22,000—**300**—32,000—10,000)

5. Into how many companies did Gideon divide his army? (1—2—**3**—300—4)

6. What picture does Scripture use to describe the number of Midianites in the valley? (like dogs—**like locusts**—like flies—like giants)

7. In which hand did the Israelites hold their torches? (**left**—right—both)

8. Who caused the men to turn their swords on each other? (Gideon—Midianites—Israel—**God**)

Applying God's Word

1. How did God show Gideon and the soldiers that their faith was not in vain? **(He gave them victory.)**

2. What did Israel do when they were in trouble? **(They asked the Lord for help.)**

3. 1 Corinthians 1:25 records, "For the foolishness of God is wiser than man's wisdom, and the weakness of God is stronger than man's strength." How does this account exemplify the truth of these New Testament words? **(God demonstrates His power at work within human weakness [2 Corinthians 12:9].)**

32 Samson (Part 1)
(Judges 13–14)

Thinking about God's Word

1. Why did the Lord give Israel over to the Philistines? Read the answer in Judges 13:1. **(Israel once again did evil in the eyes of the Lord.)**

2. What message did the angel of the Lord bring to Manoah's wife? **(She would have a son. No razor could be used on his head because he was to be a Nazirite.)** What was Manoah's son to do? **(deliver Israel from the Philistines)**

3. Whom did Samson want permission to marry? **(a Philistine woman from Timnah)** Why didn't Samson's father and mother like his marriage to a Philistine girl? **(They wanted him to marry a believer.)** Why did the Lord permit the marriage? **(He was preparing an occasion to confront the Philistines.)**

4. How did Samson show his strength when a young lion came toward him? **(He tore the lion apart with his bare hands.)** How can you tell that it really was not Samson who killed the lion? **(Judges records that the Spirit of the Lord came upon Samson.)**

5. What riddle did Samson give his companions? **(Out of the eater, something to eat; out of the strong, something sweet.)** What should Samson's wife have done when the 30 men threatened to burn her and her father's household? **(explained the whole situation to Samson)** What would you have done? **(Answers will vary.)**

Working with God's Word

Answer each question on the blank lines.
1. What did Manoah's wife name her child? **Samson**

2. Where did Samson find a wife? **among the Philistines, in Timnah**

3. To how many companions did Samson tell a riddle? **30**

4. How did Samson's wife get the answer to the riddle? **She coaxed him and cried to him for seven days.**

5. Where did Samson get the clothes to give to the men? **from 30 Philistines he killed**

Fill in the blanks with words from below.
1. Samson's father's name was **Manoah**.
2. Samson was a **Nazirite** to the Lord.
3. The **Spirit** of the Lord moved in Samson.
4. Samson went down to **Timnah**.
5. Samson tore apart the lion as he might have torn apart a **goat**.
6. Samson's riddle was answered in **seven** days.
7. Samson struck down **30** men and took their clothes.

30	seven	goat	
Nazirite	Manoah	Timnah	Spirit

Applying God's Word

1. How did Samson's wife break the Sixth Commandment? **(She went to live with Samson's friend [Judges 14:20].)**

2. What was the true source of Samson's strength? **(the Spirit of God)**

3. Compare Samson with Jesus, the ultimate Deliverer. **(Samson possessed amazing physical strength, yet Samson also demonstrated human weakness and sinfulness. Jesus was the perfect, sinless Deliverer. He single-handedly defeated the enemies of sin, death, and the devil's power so that we might be saved.)**

33 Samson (Part 2)
(Judges 15–16)

Thinking about God's Word

1. What did the Philistines do to take Samson captive? **(They threatened to fight the men of Judah.)**

2. When the Philistines shouted against Samson, what do you suppose they said? **(They probably cursed him by their gods.)**

3. What did the Philistines want Samson's wife to find out for them? **(the secret of Samson's great strength)** How did they get her to find out? **(They bribed her with shekels of silver.)**

4. What did the Philistines do to Samson? **(cut his hair, gouged out his eyes, put him in prison)**

5. Why was it easy for the Philistines to bind Samson now? **(His strength had left him.)**

6. Read the words that show that the Philistines worshiped an idol. **("The Philistines assembled to offer a great sacrifice to Dagon their god.")**

7. Who gave Samson the strength to destroy the building? **(God)** How many people in the building were killed? **(all 3,000 of them)** Which words show that Samson was killed too? **("all the people in it")**

Working with God's Word

Fill in the blanks.

1. The Philistines went up and **camped** in Judah.

2. The people of Judah bound Samson with two new **ropes**.

3. Samson struck down **1,000** men with the jawbone of a donkey.

4. Samson loved **Delilah**, a Philistine woman.

5. Samson said, "No **razor** has ever been used on my head."

6. Delilah called a man to shave off the **seven** braids of his hair.

7. The Philistines gouged out Samson's **eyes** and took him to Gaza.

8. On the roof of the temple there were about **3,000** men and women.

9. Samson took hold of the two central **pillars**.

Draw a line under the correct answer to each question.

1. Why had the Philistines come to the Israelites? (to fight—to steal—**to find Samson**—to inspect)

2. How many shekels of silver did each of the Philistine rulers promise Delilah? (**1,100**—1,200—1,300—1,400)

3. Where did the Philistines put Samson when they got to Gaza? (dungeon—grave—**prison**—house—ward)

4. Who was the god of the Philistines? (the Lord—Baal—**Dagon**—Ashtoreth)

5. How many people were on the roof of the house? (30,000—**3,000**—300—400)

Applying God's Word

1. What words indicate how Samson, like all people of God, received his strength? **("The Spirit of the LORD came upon him.")**

2. How did the Philistines break the First Commandment? How did Samson break the First Commandment? **(The Philistines worshiped the false god Dagon. Samson allowed his relationship with Delilah to interfere with his relationship with God.)**

3. In his death Samson destroyed much evil. How does Samson's death remind us of the death of Jesus? **(Whereas Samson destroyed more of the enemy in death than he did in life, when Jesus died He defeated the forces of unholy trinity—sin, death, and Satan's power.)**

34 Ruth

(The Book of Ruth)

Thinking about God's Word

1. When did the famine mentioned in our lesson come over Canaan? See Ruth 1:1. **(during the time of the judges)**

2. How many persons belonged to the family of Elimelech? **(6)**

3. Whom did Elimelech's sons marry? **(Moabite women—Ruth and Orpah)**

4. After 10 years in the land of Moab, who of Elimelech's family were still living? **(Naomi, Ruth, and Orpah)**

5. To which land did Naomi now want to return? **(Judah)** What did Ruth answer when Naomi told her daughters-in-law to return to their own homes? **("Where you go I will go, and where you stay I will stay. Your people will be my people and your God my God.")**

6. After the two women settled in Bethlehem, where did Ruth work to provide food for Naomi and herself? **(in the fields of Boaz)**

7. Who was Boaz? **(a distant relative of Elimelech)** How did he show favor to Ruth? **(He intentionally left grain for her to pick up.)** Why did he favor her? **(He had heard about her kindness to Naomi.)** Whose property did Boaz buy? **(Elimelech's)**

8. Who was Ruth's grandson? **(Jesse)** Who was her great-grandson? **(David)**

Working with God's Word

Answer each question with one word.

1. Who took his wife and two sons to Moab? **Elimelech**

2. Where did the wives of Mahlon and Kilion come from? **Moab**

3. To which town did Ruth and Naomi go? **Bethlehem**

4. Who owned fields in Bethlehem? **Boaz**

5. Who became the wife of Boaz? **Ruth**

6. Who was Jesse's son? **David**

7. What was the relationship of Ruth to David? **great-grandmother**

Draw a line under the word that makes each sentence true.

1. Naomi was the wife of (**Elimelech**—Mahlon—Kilion—Boaz).

2. Elimelech had (2—3—4—5) sons.

3. Naomi was Ruth's (sister-in-law—daughter-in-law—**mother-in-law**).

4. Naomi lived in Moab about (5—**10**—15—20) years.

5. (Ruth—**Orpah**—Delilah—Miriam) left Naomi to return to her mother's house.

6. Boaz lived in (**Bethlehem**—Moab—Jerusalem—Jericho).

7. (Ruth—Orpah—Naomi—**Boaz**) was Ruth's second husband.

Applying God's Word

1. Ruth's words to Naomi include a beautiful confession of faith. Explain. **(Ruth says that the God of Naomi is her God also.)**

2. How does the story of Ruth show us that God's love and grace extend to all people? **(Ruth was a Moabite, and therefore she was not born into the people of God. Yet God's kingdom extended to her. Ruth became an ancestor of the Savior of the world.)**

3. Ruth became the ancestor of many kings, including King David. Who is Ruth's greatest descendant? See Matthew 1:1–5. **(Jesus, the King of kings)**

35 The Boy Samuel
(1 Samuel 1–4)

Thinking about God's Word

1. Read 1 Samuel 1:10–11. Why was Hannah, the wife of Elkanah, "in bitterness of soul"? **(She had no children.)**

2. To whom did she pray? **(to the Lord)**

3. What promise did Hannah make to the Lord? **(She would give her son to Him.)**

4. How did the Lord remember Hannah? **(He gave her a son.)**

5. What did Hannah name her child? **(Samuel)** How did she keep her promise? **(She brought young Samuel to Eli, so he could minister there with him.)**

Working with God's Word

Answer each question.

1. Who were Elkanah's two wives? **Hannah and Peninnah**

2. Why did Hannah pray to the Lord? **She had no children.**

3. Why did Hannah bring Samuel to the house of the Lord? **to give him back to the Lord**

4. How was the Lord going to punish Eli and his sons? **Eli's two sons would die on the same day**.

5. What did the Lord tell Samuel while he slept? **"I will carry out against Eli everything I spoke against his family."**

6. Against whom did Israel go to battle? **the Philistines**

7. What happened to the Israelites? **Israel fled before the Philistines, and their army suffered heavy losses.**

8. What happened to Eli and his two sons? **The sons died in battle on the same day; Eli died when he heard the news.**

Draw a line through the sentences that are not true.

1. Elkanah had a wife by the name of Hannah.

2. Peninnah was the wife of Elkanah.

3. ~~Hannah called her son Eli.~~

4. ~~Eli was a good father.~~

5. Eli was Samuel's teacher.

6. God said to Eli, "Your two sons will both die on the same day."

7. The Philistines took the ark of God.

Applying God's Word

1. How does this account show that children are a gift of God? **(Hannah prayed for a son, and God granted her request. Later, God blessed Hannah with other children.)**

2. According to the man of God, what sin did Eli commit? **(Eli honored his sons more than he honored God.)**

3. How did Hannah show that she loved God even more than she loved her son? **(Hannah dedicated her son to the Lord and took him to serve God in the temple.)**

36 King Saul

(1 Samuel 8–15)

Thinking about God's Word

1. Who was the last judge of Israel? See 1 Samuel 7:15. **(Samuel)**

2. Why did the elders tell Samuel they wanted a king? **(The other nations had kings.)** Why was that a sin? **(They were rejecting God as their King.)**

3. Why did Samuel call the tribes of Israel together? **(to select a king)** Note: There were 13 tribes in Israel, one for each son of Jacob except Joseph. He was honored with two tribes named after his two sons, Ephraim and Manasseh. We usually speak of 12 tribes because the sons of Levi did not inherit a province of their own. They were the priests and as such received offerings from the other tribes.

4. How did Saul, the new king, show his humility? **(He hid among the baggage.)**

5. Why did Saul immediately have to go to war? **(Nahash the Ammonite besieged Jabesh Gilead.)** What two things made it possible for Saul to win? **(The Spirit of God came upon Saul in power, and the terror of the Lord fell upon the people.)** Why? **(God controlled the events.)**

Working with God's Word

Answer each question with one word or a short phrase.

1. Who came to Samuel and asked for a king? **the elders of Israel**

2. Whom had Israel rejected? **God**

3. Who was chosen as Israel's first king? **Saul**

4. Who came upon Saul? **the Spirit of God**

5. Who won the battle against Ammon? **Israel by the power of God**

6. What instructions regarding the Amalekites did God give Saul? **destroy everything**

7. Whose instructions did Saul say he performed? **God's**

8. What had Saul spared besides the sheep? **cattle, everything that was good**

9. What is not as important as obedience? **sacrifice**

Of whom do you think when you read each of the following sentences?

1. All the elders of Israel came to him. **Samuel**

2. He was displeased that Israel wanted a king. **Samuel**

3. The first king was the son of Kish. **Saul**

4. They shouted, "Long live the king." **people of Israel**

5. He said, "I did what the LORD wanted." **Saul**

6. He said, "To obey is better than sacrifice." **Samuel**

7. He rejected Saul as king. **God**

Applying God's Word

1. What does this account teach us about the relationship between God and our governing authorities? **(Our governing authorities are God's gifts to us.)**

2. Evaluate Saul's words "I have carried out the LORD's instructions." **(Saul had not really obeyed God. He justified not following God's directions by saying he had spared some of the sheep and cattle to be sacrificed to God, but Saul had disobeyed God nonetheless.)**

3. How do God's people rightly honor Him as Lord of their lives? See Acts 5:29. **(God requires obedience to Him, even over and above our obedience to the authorities He has placed over us.)**

37 David Is Chosen
(1 Samuel 16–17)

Thinking about God's Word

1. Why did the Lord send Samuel to Jesse? **(God had chosen one of Jesse's sons to be king.)**

2. Read the words that tell that David was blessed and Saul was plagued. **("The Spirit of the LORD came upon David. The Spirit of the LORD had departed from Saul, and an evil spirit tormented him.")**

3. Against whom did Saul and his army have to go to battle again? **(Philistines)**

4. Why, do you suppose, was Goliath so eager to fight this battle alone with an Israelite? **(He was anxious to demonstrate his unusual strength and his confidence in victory.)** In whom did the giant put his trust? **(himself)** In whom should Israel have trusted? **(the Lord)**

5. How did David show that he was not frightened by the giant? **(David asked, "Who is this uncircumcised Philistine that he should defy the armies of the living God?")**

Working with God's Word

Write the answers to the following questions.

1. Who was chosen to be the next king? **David**

2. How can you tell that God was with David? **God's Spirit came upon him.**

3. Who gathered their armies against Israel? **Philistines**

4. Who was the champion of the Philistines? **Goliath**

5. Who was afraid of him? **Saul and the Israelite army**

6. How did David help his father? **David tended his father's sheep.**

7. What did David call the Philistine giant? **this uncircumcised Philistine**

8. To whom were the words of David reported? **Saul**

Answer Yes or No.

1. Did David play a violin for Saul?   Yes   **No**

2. Did David serve the king?   **Yes**   No

3. Was Goliath more than 10 feet tall?   Yes   **No**

4. Were Saul and his army afraid of Goliath? **Yes**   No

5. Did Goliath come forward every day for 40 days? **Yes**   No

6. Was David afraid of Goliath?   Yes   **No**

7. Did David trust in himself?   Yes   **No**

Applying God's Word

1. How did God give David opportunity to learn the work of a king? **(David played his harp for Saul, becoming part of the king's household.)**

2. What evidence shows that God's Spirit was upon David? **(David was angry at Goliath's defiance of the armies of the living God.)**

3. How do the words of David's most famous psalm, Psalm 23, reflect his background as a musician, shepherd, and soldier? **(David used his musicianship to praise God with the psalm, which was written to be set to music. In the psalm He calls the Lord his shepherd and thinks of himself as a sheep. As a soldier, David many times would have found himself in danger, walking through the valley of the shadow of death. David trusted in God's loving protection and care.)**

38 David and Goliath
(1 Samuel 17)

Thinking about God's Word

1. How did David prove to Saul that he was not afraid of the giant? **(He offered to fight him.)**

2. Why didn't David take the armor of Saul? **(David was not accustomed to armor.)** Describe the weapons he did take. **(David took a sling, a staff, and a bag containing five smooth stones.)**

3. Which words of Goliath show that he despised David? **("Am I a dog, that you come at me with sticks?")**

4. With what did Goliath come to David? **(sword, spear, and javelin)** In whose name did David come to Goliath? **(the name of the Lord Almighty, the God of the armies of Israel)** Who was better prepared? **(David)** Why? **(David relied on God for victory.)**

5. How did David boldly foretell who would win? **(David said, "This day the LORD will hand you over to me, and the whole world will know that there is a God in Israel.")** Why would God hand Goliath over to David? **(to show His power and love for His people)**

6. How did David drop the giant to the ground? **(He hit Goliath in the forehead with a stone.)** How did David kill him? **(David cut off his head.)**

7. Why did the Philistines flee? **(They saw that their hero was dead.)** Why was it easy for Israel to win now? **(They knew God was on their side; the Philistines' champion was dead.)**

Working with God's Word

Answer each question.

1. When Goliath appeared, what did David say to Saul? **"Your servant will go and fight him."**

2. Why didn't Saul think David could win? **David was only a boy facing a mighty and seasoned warrior.**

3. Why did David know he could win? **David knew God would help him.**

4. How did Saul wish to protect David? **Saul encouraged David to use his armor.**

5. What things did David use for weapons? **staff, sling, and five smooth stones**

6. What attitude did David show in his words to Goliath? **his trust in God**

7. Where did the stone strike the giant? **in the forehead**

8. How did David make sure that Goliath would die? **He cut off his head.**

9. Who won the battle? **Israelites**

Are the following sentences true or false?

1. Saul commanded David to fight Goliath. T **F**

2. David belonged to the army of Israel. T **F**

3. With the Lord, David could not be beaten. **T** F

4. David was a soldier of the Lord. **T** F

5. David chose five smooth stones. **T** F

6. David carried no real weapon of war. **T** F

7. Goliath trusted in himself. **T** F

8. Goliath trusted in his sword, shield, and spear. **T** F

9. The Lord won the war for Israel. **T** F

10. The First Commandment tells us to trust in God above all things. **T** F

Applying God's Word

1. What was David's answer to Saul's words? **("The LORD will deliver me from the hand of this Philistine.")** How did David know that the Lord would deliver him? Think of what he had received from Samuel. **(God's Spirit was upon David.)**

2. What important lesson did David teach the army of Israel? **(trust in God)**

3. David faced and defeated Israel's great enemy. Some thousand years later, David's descendant defeated the greatest enemy of all people. Explain. **(On our behalf, Jesus defeated sin and the powers of evil so that we might be saved.)**

39 David's Fall and Repentance
(2 Samuel 11–12)

Thinking about God's Word

1. Who really killed Uriah? **(David)** Why? **(He arranged for his death.)**

2. Why did the Lord send Nathan to David? **(to convict David of his sin)** Read what Nathan said to him.

3. If David meant what he said about punishing the rich man, whom would he have had to punish? **(himself)** How was David punished? **(The son born to David and Bathsheba died.)**

4. Which were David's words of repentance? **("I have sinned against the LORD.")**

5. In which words did Nathan announce God's forgiveness to David? **("The LORD has taken away your sin. You are not going to die.")**

Working with God's Word

Answer each question with one word.

1. Whom did Joab and his servants destroy? **Uriah**

2. At what time of day did David walk upon the roof of his palace? **evening**

3. Whose wife was Bathsheba? **Uriah's**

4. Whom did David take to be his wife? **Bathsheba**

5. Who was the man who took the poor man's lamb? **David**

6. What had David done against God? **sinned**

7. Was David's sin forgiven? **yes**

Fill in the blanks with words from below.

David sent **Joab** to fight against Ammon and Rabbah, while he stayed in **Jerusalem**. David wanted Bathsheba's husband to **die**. After Uriah was dead, David took Bathsheba to be his **wife**. David said, "I have **sinned** against the LORD." David's sin was **forgiven** but his child **died**.

Nathan	sinned	died
wife	sin	Joab
Jerusalem	die	forgiven

Applying God's Word

1. Where should David have been instead of at home in Jerusalem? **(with his army)** How did Satan use David's idleness to lead him into sin? **(David gave in to temptation and sinned.)**

2. Explain the truth about David's words after hearing Nathan's story of the rich man's theft. **(David was correct in his judgment that the man who committed the offense deserved to die.)**

3. What words reveal God's grace to David? **(Nathan said, "The LORD has taken away your sin. You are not going to die.")** Who took away David's sin and ours? **(Jesus paid for all sins—those of David as well as ours.)**

40 Absalom's Rebellion

(2 Samuel 14–18)

Thinking about God's Word

1. Who was Absalom? **(David's son)** For what was he praised? **(his handsome appearance)**

2. What did Absalom want? **(He wanted to be king.)** Why was this a sin? See Romans 13:9. **(Absalom was dishonoring both his father and his government.)**

3. How did Absalom steal the hearts of the Israelites? **(He told the people he would see things their way if he were king.)**

4. What did Absalom tell his father he wanted in Hebron? **(to fulfill a vow to the Lord)** Which words showed that he wanted to start a rebellion? **("As soon as you hear the sound of the trumpets, then say, 'Absalom is king in Hebron.' ")** Find the meaning of the word *rebellion* in your dictionary. **(A rebellion is an uprising against a ruling body of authority.)**

5. Who fled from his son? **(David)** Who chased after his father? **(Absalom)**

Working with God's Word

Fill in the blanks with the correct word.

1. Absalom said, "If only I were appointed **judge** in the land."

2. Absalom said that he wanted to go to Hebron to fulfill a **vow**.

3. David had to **flee** from Absalom, his son.

4. Joab killed Absalom with three **javelins**.

5. Absalom was buried in a **pit**.

Draw a line under the word or phrase that makes each sentence true.

1. David was Absalom's (brother—**father**—servant—general).

2. Absalom said he wanted to go to (Jerusalem—Jordan—Bethlehem—**Hebron**) to fulfill a vow.

3. Despising the government is sinning against the (Third—**Fourth**—Ninth—Tenth) Commandment.

4. David and his people fled across the (Nile—Kishon—**Jordan**—Tigris).

5. Absalom fled (**on a mule**—on a horse—in a chariot—in a wagon).

6. Absalom's head caught in the boughs of (a maple—a pine—**an oak**—a sycamore).

7. Absalom's body was covered with (earth—**stones**—water—grass).

Applying God's Word

1. How did the father show his love for his son in spite of his son's unfaithfulness? **(David ordered his soldiers to be gentle with Absalom for his sake.)**

2. Absalom not only rebelled against his father, but he also rebelled against God. Explain. **(Absalom disobeyed God by not giving David the honor due him as his father and king.)**

3. Which commandment did Absalom clearly break? Who kept this and all other commandments for us? **(Absalom clearly disobeyed the commandment "Honor your father and your mother." Jesus kept this and all other commandments for us.)**

41

Solomon and the Temple
(1 Kings 3–8)

Thinking about God's Word

1. Who was Solomon's father? **(David)**

2. What special favor did Solomon ask for? **(a wise and discerning heart to govern well)**

3. What did the Lord give Solomon that was more than he asked for? **(riches, honor, and a long life)**

4. What should Solomon do to have a long life? **(walk in God's ways)**

5. What did Solomon build? **(a temple)**

6. How long did it take to build? **(seven years)**

7. What did Solomon ask the Lord to do for the people of Israel? **(answer their prayers)**

Working with God's Word

Answer each question correctly.

1. Who sat upon the throne of David, his father? **Solomon**

2. How did the Lord appear to Solomon? **in a dream**

3. What did the Lord give Solomon? **wisdom, honor, and riches**

4. Who said the prayer before the altar of the Lord? **Solomon**

5. What did Solomon ask the Lord to do for those who sinned against Him? **forgive them**

Draw a line under the word or phrase that answers the question correctly.

1. What did Solomon call himself before the Lord? (king—priest—**servant**—man)

2. What did Solomon pray for? (honor—riches—**wisdom**—a great kingdom)

3. Where was the ark of the covenant placed? (in the palace—**in the Most Holy Place**—in the court)

4. What name did Solomon call God in his prayer? (Jehovah—God—Almighty—**Lord, God of Israel**)

Applying God's Word

1. What portion of Solomon's answer to God indicates his humility and faith? **(Solomon said, "O LORD, I am only a little child and do not know how to carry out my duties. So give Your servant a discerning heart to govern Your people and to distinguish between right and wrong.")**

2. With what action did Solomon demonstrate his love for God? **(Solomon built the Lord a beautiful temple; it required seven years of construction.)**

3. How did Solomon show his concern for the sins of his people? **(Solomon prayed, asking that God would hear the prayers of the people and forgive their sins.)** Who ultimately paid for the sins of all people? How much did it cost? **(Jesus paid for the sins of all people; it cost Him His very life.)**

42

The Prophet Elijah
(1 Kings 16–17)

Thinking about God's Word

1. Ahab was the seventh king of Israel. Which words tell that he was very wicked? **(Ahab began to serve Baal and did more to provoke the God of Israel than did all the kings of Israel before him.)**

2. How did the Lord try to bring Ahab to repentance? **(He sent a drought.)**

3. Why was "neither dew nor rain" a terrible punishment? **(Soon there would be no food.)** How long would the curse last? **(for a few years)** Which words tell that rain would fall again only at God's command? **("except at My word")**

4. How did the Lord take care of His servant Elijah? **(Ravens brought Elijah food. Later the widow at Zarephath provided for him.)** Why? **(God cares for His people.)**

5. Why was it not only a miracle that food was brought to Elijah, but also that *ravens* brought the food? **(There was little food; birds don't usually bring people food.)**

6. Why did Elijah leave the brook in the Kerith Ravine? **(The brook dried up.)**

7. Why was it strange that the Lord should command a widow to feed His prophet? **(Widows were usually the ones in need of help.)**

8. Why was Elijah's request for water hard to grant? **(She had to go and get it.)**

9. Why would this widow not have to fear? **(God promised to provide for her.)** How can you tell that she believed? **(She did as Elijah said.)**

10. How was Elijah able to bring the widow's son back from death? **(Elijah prayed to God, and God returned the boy to life.)**

Working with God's Word

Fill in the blanks.

1. Ahab sinned against God by worshiping **Baal.**

2. **Elijah** the prophet talked to Ahab.

3. God held back **dew and rain** from Ahab's land.

4. Ravens brought Elijah **bread** and meat.

5. The Lord told Elijah to go to the city of **Zarephath.**

6. A **widow** took care of Elijah in this city.

7. **God** gives us all our food.

Draw a line through the sentences that are not true.

1. ~~God sent rain to the earth when Ahab asked for it.~~

2. The Lord commanded Elijah to hide at the Kerith Ravine.

3. Ravens brought food in the morning and evening to Elijah.

4. ~~Elijah went to the home of a widow in Zebulon.~~

5. ~~Elijah gathered sticks near the village of Zarephath.~~

6. ~~The Lord gave the widow money to buy food.~~

7. ~~Elijah brought the widow's husband back from the dead.~~

Applying God's Word

1. Of which Sacrament do the miracles of God's care for Elijah remind us? **(The miracles of the feeding of Elijah remind us of the miraculous way God provides for our spiritual nourishment through the Sacrament of the Altar.)**

2. How does God's care for Elijah compare with God's care for us? **(God daily provides us with everything we need for the care and support of our bodies.)**

3. What other Bible accounts show God's power over death? **(Possibilities include Jesus' raising of the young man of Nain, the daughter of Jairus, Lazarus, and Jesus' own resurrection from the dead.)**

43 Elijah and the Prophets of Baal
(1 Kings 18)

Thinking about God's Word

1. Whom were the people worshiping besides God? **(Baal)**

2. How did Elijah put the idol Baal to a test? **(Two altars with sacrifices were prepared, one for Baal and one for the true God. The one who set fire to the sacrifice would be regarded as the true God.)**

3. What showed that the idol Baal had no power? **(Baal's altar remained without fire.)**

4. How did Elijah make it harder for fire to burn his altar? **(Elijah drenched the altar to the true God with water.)** On whom did he call? **(God)**

5. How can you tell that the fire that fell from heaven was truly a fire sent by God? **(It was supernatural fire; it even consumed the water and stones.)**

6. How did the people confess that Elijah had won the test? **(They fell prostrate and cried, "The LORD—He is God! The LORD—He is God!")**

7. What did the people now do at Elijah's command? **(They seized and executed the prophets of Baal.)**

Working with God's Word

Draw a line through the following sentences that are not taken from the story.

1. Elijah said, "Get two bulls for us."
2. ~~They called on Dagon all day long.~~
3. ~~He repaired the altar of the Lord that was broken down.~~
4. ~~Elijah took 12 stones and built an altar.~~
5. He dug a trench around the altar.
6. The water ran down around the altar and even filled the trench.
7. "Answer me, O LORD; answer me!"
8. Then the fire of the Lord fell and burned up the sacrifice.

Fill in the blanks with words from below.

Elijah preached to the people. He said, "If the LORD is God, follow Him; but if **Baal** is God, follow him." The prophets of Baal prepared a **bull**. Elijah did likewise. Then the prophets of Baal called to Baal from **morning** till noon. But Baal did not answer. When Elijah prayed to the Lord, fire fell from **heaven**. It burned the bull, the wood, the stones, and the soil and licked up the **water**. The people then fell down and **praised** God. But Elijah took the prophets of Baal to the **Kishon** Valley and slaughtered them.

heaven	Baal	LORD
morning	water	bull
praised	Kishon	fire
Elijh		

Applying God's Word

1. Elijah exemplifies the courage God gives His people. Explain. **(Empowered by God, Elijah stood faithfully alone against hundreds of prophets of the false god Baal.)**

2. Why can it always be said that the power to believe comes down from heaven? **(God is the only source of the power to believe. He works faith in us through the means of grace.)**

3. Elijah prayed to the God of Abraham, Isaac, and Israel. Is Elijah's God the same as ours? Explain. **(There is and always has been only one true God. The God of Abraham, Isaac, and Israel is also our God.)**

44 Naboth's Vineyard
(1 Kings 21)

Thinking about God's Word

1. For what purpose did Ahab say he wanted Naboth's vineyard? **(He wanted to use it as a garden.)** How did he intend to get it? **(He offered to buy it or to trade for it.)**

2. Why would it have been a sin for Naboth to trade or sell his land? See Numbers 36:7. **(It was his inheritance. Numbers 36:7 records, "No inheritance in Israel is to pass from tribe to tribe, for every Israelite shall keep the tribal land inherited from his forefathers.")**

3. How did the king act like a small child? **(He became sullen and angry; he sulked and refused to eat.)**

4. Who was Jezebel? **(The queen, Ahab's wife)** What promise did she make to the king? **(Jezebel promised she would get the vineyard for Ahab.)**

5. What was her scheme for getting the vineyard? **(She would get Naboth falsely accused, convicted, and executed so the king could take possession of his property.)**

6. Why was Ahab able to take possession of the vineyard? **(Naboth was dead.)**

7. What was Elijah to say to Ahab? **("This is what the LORD says: Have you not murdered a man and seized his property? In the place where dogs licked up Naboth's blood, dogs will lick up your blood! Dogs will devour Jezebel by the wall of Jezreel. Dogs will eat those belonging to Ahab who die in the city, and the birds of the air will feed on those who die in the country.")**

Working with God's Word

Answer each question.

1. Where was Naboth's vineyard? **close to the palace of the king of Samaria**

2. Why couldn't Naboth sell his vineyard? **It was inherited from his forefathers.**

3. Who said she would get the vineyard? **Jezebel**

4. What were the false witnesses to say against Naboth? **Naboth cursed both God and the king.**

5. How was Naboth put to death? **He was stoned.**

6. Whom did the Lord send to Ahab? **Elijah the prophet**

7. Where would Ahab die? **where Naboth died**

8. Where and how would Jezebel die? **Jezebel would die by the wall of Jezreel; she would be thrown from a building.**

9. Which words say that Elijah's words came true? **"And all of it happened as the word of the LORD had declared."**

Draw a line under the correct answer to each question.

1. Coveting is a sin against which commandment? (Seventh—Fifth—**Ninth**—Eighth)

2. How had Naboth gotten his property? (bought it—earned it—**inherited it**—stole it)

3. To whom were the letters sent? (priests—**elders**—princes—soldiers)

4. False witnesses sin against which commandment? (Seventh—Fifth—Ninth—**Eighth**)

5. Whom did dogs eat? (**Jezebel**—Naboth—Elijah—Ahab)

Applying God's Word

1. To what other sins may coveting lead, as illustrated by this Bible story? **(Coveting can lead to lying, stealing, and murder.)**

2. What does this account show about God's attitude toward sin? **(God punishes sin. Note God's judgment against Ahab and Jezebel.)**

3. How did God solve the problem of human sinfulness? **(God sent His only Son to pay for the sins of the world.)**

45 Elisha Sees Elijah Ascend

(2 Kings 2)

Thinking about God's Word

1. How was the Lord going to take Elijah into heaven? **(in a whirlwind)**

2. Who went with Elijah to cross the River Jordan? **(Elisha)** How did they get across? **(Elijah struck the water with his cloak, the water divided, and the two crossed on dry ground.)**

3. Elijah was Elisha's teacher. After Elijah ascended into heaven, Elisha was to be prophet in his place. How did Elisha's answer to his teacher show that he knew what gift he needed to serve in Elijah's place? **(Elisha asked for a double portion of Elijah's spirit.)**

4. What form of transportation did the angels of heaven use to get Elijah? **(a chariot and horses of fire)**

5. Who saw this miracle? **(Elisha)** What did he call after Elijah? **("My father! My father! The chariots and horsemen of Israel!")**

6. By what miracle did the Lord show Elisha that He was with him? **(He divided the water when Elisha used Elijah's cloak, just as Elijah had done.)**

7. What did the prophets of Jericho now say of Elisha? **("The spirit of Elijah is resting on Elisha.")** What did they mean? **(Elisha was to take Elijah's place.)** How did they know? See 2 Kings 2:14–15. **(They saw Elisha part the River Jordan as Elijah had done.)**

Working with God's Word

Answer each question with one word or a short phrase.

1. Where did the Lord want to take Elijah? **heaven**

2. Who walked with Elijah? **Elisha**

3. With what did Elijah hit the water? **cloak**

4. For how big a portion of Elijah's spirit did Elisha ask? **a double portion**

5. In what did Elijah ride to heaven? **in a chariot pulled by horses of fire in a whirlwind**

Answer each question with Yes or No.

1. Was Elijah a true servant of God? **Yes** No

2. Did the waters part for Elijah? **Yes** No

3. Did Elijah ask for a double portion of Elisha's spirit? Yes **No**

4. Did Elijah go up by a whirlwind to heaven? **Yes** No

5. Did Elisha cry, "My father! My father! The chariots and horsemen of Israel!"? **Yes** No

6. Did Elisha strike the waters with his cloak? Yes **No**

7. Did the prophets live in Bethel? Yes **No**

Applying God's Word

1. Why did Elisha refer to Elijah as his father? **(Elijah taught Elisha about God.)** Who has taught you about God? **(Answers will vary.)**

2. How do you know that you have received the Holy Spirit (1 Corinthians 12:3)? **(If we have faith, we have the Holy Spirit. No one comes to faith outside of the working of the Holy Spirit.)**

3. Elijah preceded Elisha. Who similarly preceded Jesus to prepare the way for Him and His atoning ministry (see Luke 1:17 and John 1:29–34)? **(John the Baptist was the forerunner of Jesus.)**

46 Naaman and Elisha
(2 Kings 5)

Thinking about God's Word

1. Who was Naaman? **(commander of the army of the king of Aram)**

2. What was wrong with him? **(He had leprosy.)**

3. What did the servant girl say? **("If only my master would see the prophet who is in Samaria!")**

4. Why did Naaman take money and clothing to Samaria? **(as gifts)** How did he travel? **(with horses and chariots)**

5. How did Elisha humble Naaman? **(He sent a messenger to tell Naaman to wash seven times in the Jordan River.)**

6. How did the servants persuade their master to try Elisha's cure? **(They reasoned, "My father, if the prophet had told you to do some great thing, would you not have done it?" And so they persuaded him.)** What happened? **(Naaman did as Elisha said, and he was cured.)**

7. In which words did Naaman admit that God of Israel had cured him? **("Now I know that there is no God in all the world except in Israel.")** How did he want to reward Elisha? **(with a gift)** Why do you suppose Elisha refused the reward? **(The healing came not from Elisha, but from the Lord.)**

Working with God's Word

Fill in the blanks.

1. **Naaman** was commander of the army of the king of Aram.

2. **Naaman** had leprosy.

3. A **young girl from Israel** served Naaman's wife.

4. Naaman was told to wash in the **Jordan** River seven times.

5. Naaman thought the rivers of **Damascus** were better than the rivers of Israel.

6. **Gehazi** was a servant of Elisha.

7. Naaman gave Gehazi **two** talents of silver.

8. Gehazi said to Elisha, "Your servant **didn't** go anywhere."

9. Gehazi became a **leper**.

Draw a line through the sentences that are not true.

1. ~~Naaman was king of Syria.~~

2. A servant girl told Naaman to go to Samaria.

3. Naaman took much gold, silver, and clothing on his trip to Samaria.

4. Elisha did not go out to see Naaman when he came to Samaria to be healed.

5. ~~Naaman dipped himself into the Jordan River six times.~~

6. Naaman became a believer in the true God.

7. ~~Gehazi was Naaman's servant.~~

8. Gehazi was punished for coveting, lying, and deceiving.

Applying God's Word

1. What evidence does this account provide of God's love and grace for all people? **(God blessed Naaman with His healing grace, even though Naaman was not of the people of Israel.)**

2. What does this account teach us about God's attitude toward sin? **(God punishes sin. Gehazi lied in order to extract gifts from Naaman. He became a leper.)**

3. Naaman's washing in the Jordan reminds us of the Baptism God offers us in Christ Jesus. Explain. **(Through faith in Jesus, Baptism washes away our sin.)**

47 God Sends Jonah

(Jonah 1–3)

Thinking about God's Word

1. Who was Jonah? **(son of Amittai)**

2. Where did the Lord tell Jonah to go? **(to Nineveh)** Why? **(to preach to the people, telling them to repent of their great wickedness)**

3. Why did Jonah get on a ship? **(He planned to run away from the Lord by sailing to Tarshish.)**

4. Whom was Jonah trying to get away from? **(the Lord)**

5. What did Jonah tell the sailors to do? **(Throw him into the sea.)**

6. Where was Jonah for three days and three nights? **(in the belly of a great fish)**

7. How did Jonah survive? **(Jonah prayed to God, and God helped Jonah.)**

Working with God's Word

Fill in the blanks with words from below.

1. Jonah said, "Pick me up and throw me into the **sea**."

2. A great **fish** swallowed Jonah.

3. Jonah prayed, "In my distress I called to the **Lord**."

4. The Lord told Jonah to go to the city of **Nineveh**.

5. The people of Nineveh were **wicked**.

6. The people of Nineveh would be overturned in **40** days.

7. The Ninevites declared a **fast**.

8. The Ninevites put on **sackcloth**.

fast	sackcloth	wicked
fish	sea	40
30	Lord	Nineveh

Draw a line under the word that makes each sentence true.

1. Jonah was the son of (David—Micah—**Amittai**—Joshua).

2. The great city of Nineveh was (good—**wicked**—new—poor).

3. The Lord sent a (**wind**—rainbow—boat—sailor) on the sea.

4. When Jonah was thrown overboard, the sea grew (choppy—**calm**—rough—deep).

5. God had (vengeance—pity—**compassion**—mercy) on the people in the city.

Applying God's Word

1. By sending Jonah to Nineveh, how did God demonstrate His desire to save all people? **(The people of Nineveh were Gentiles. God saved them also through the ministry of Jonah.)**

2. How is God's salvation for the people of Nineveh like the salvation He offers to us? **(Though, like the people of Nineveh, we deserve nothing but punishment and eternal destruction, God has rescued us through Jesus, our Savior.)**

3. In what way are the story of Jonah and the story of Jesus the same? **(Just as Jonah was inside the fish for three days, Jesus was in the tomb until the third day.)**

48 Jeremiah

(Jeremiah 37–38)

Thinking about God's Word

1. What did Jeremiah tell the king of Judah? **("Pharaoh's army, which has marched out to support you, will go back to its own land, to Egypt. Then the Babylonians will return and attack this city; they will capture it and burn it down.")**

2. What did the officials say to the king? **("This man should be put to death. He is discouraging the soldiers who are left in this city, as well as all the people, by the things he is saying to them. This man is not seeking the good of these people but their ruin.")**

3. Where did the officials put Jeremiah? **(into a cistern)**

4. What did Ebed-Melech say to the king? **("My lord the king, these men have acted wickedly in all they have done to Jeremiah the prophet. They have thrown him into a cistern, where he will starve to death when there is no longer any bread in the city.")**

5. How did they save him? **(They took old rags and worn-out clothes and told Jeremiah to put them under his arms for pads; then they pulled Jeremiah out of the cistern using ropes.)**

Working with God's Word

Fill in each blank with one word.

1. According to God's Word to Jeremiah, this ally of Judah would return home instead of coming to Judah's aid. **Egypt**

2. **Zedekiah** was king of Judah.

3. God told Jeremiah that **Babylonians** would attack and burn down the city.

4. Lowered into the cistern, Jeremiah sank into the **mud.**

5. The king commanded his official to take **30** men with him and lift Jeremiah out of the cistern.

Put a line through the sentences that are not true.

1. Jeremiah was a prophet.

2. Jeremiah was to tell the king, "Pharaoh's army . . . will go back to its own land, to Egypt."

3. ~~The Amorites were going to return to attack the city.~~

4. ~~Jeremiah spoke to King Hezekiah.~~

5. ~~They put Jeremiah into a stream.~~

Applying God's Word

1. Why was Jeremiah's message unpopular? When is God's Word unpopular today? **(Jeremiah's message was discouraging. Similarly God's Word can be unpopular today among those who only want to hear messages of forthcoming earthly prosperity.)**

2. In what way did God bless Jeremiah through Ebed-Melech? **(Ebed-Melech spoke to the king on Jeremiah's behalf; as a result, some men rescued Jeremiah.)**

3. How is Jeremiah's release from the cistern similar to Jesus' release from the tomb? How is it different? **(After being imprisoned in a cistern, Jeremiah was freed. Jesus was dead and laid in the tomb. He left the tomb after God raised Him from the dead on Easter morning. Others helped Jeremiah out of the tomb. Jesus escaped death and the tomb with His own power.)**

49 The Three Men in the Fiery Furnace
(Daniel 3)

Thinking about God's Word

1. How did Nebuchadnezzar sin against the First Commandment? **(He made an image out of gold and commanded the people to worship it.)** Whom did he gather to come to the dedication? **(the provincial officials)**

2. How did the king force the people to commit idolatry? **(He commanded the people to worship the image whenever they heard music.)** How did he threaten to punish them if they disobeyed? **(Those who refused would be thrown into a blazing furnace.)**

3. Who did not obey the command of the king? **(Shadrach, Meshach, and Abednego)**

4. What did the king say to the three men? **("If you do not worship my image, you will be thrown immediately into a blazing furnace. Then what god will be able to rescue you from my hand?")** What did they answer? **("If we are thrown into the blazing furnace, the God we serve is able to save us from it. But even if He does not, we want you to know, O king, that we will not worship the image of gold.")**

5. Were the three men sure that God *could* save them? **(Yes)** Give a reason. **(They confessed their faith in God.)** Did the three men know whether or not God *wanted* to save them? **(No)** Give a reason. **(They said they would not worship the image even if God refused to save them.)**

6. Why was Nebuchadnezzar astonished when he looked into the furnace? **(He saw four men walking around in the furnace.)** What did he say? **("Weren't there three men that we tied up and threw into the fire? Look! I see four men walking around in the fire, unbound and unharmed, and the fourth looks like a son of the gods.")**

7. What words show that the men were not hurt? **(Not a hair of their heads was singed; their robes were not scorched, and there was no smell of fire on them.)**

8. How did the king now confess that the Lord was stronger than he? **(He said, "Praise be to the God of Shadrach, Meshach and Abednego, who has sent His angel and rescued His servants who trusted in Him.")**

Working with God's Word

Answer each question on the blank lines.

1. What did King Nebuchadnezzar have made of gold? **an image**

2. Why did he have the image made? **He wanted an idol for the people to worship.**

3. How were those who did not worship the image to be punished? **They were to be thrown into a blazing furnace.**

4. Why did the king have the furnace made seven times hotter? **He was furious with the three men.**

5. What was done with the three men before they were thrown into the furnace? **They were tied up.**

6. Who was the fourth man in the furnace? **an angel**

7. Why do you think he had gone into the flames? **to show God's protection for the three faithful men**

Draw a line under the correct answer to each question.

1. Of what was the idol made?
   (silver—**gold**—brass—iron)

2. What gave the signal for worshiping the idol?
   (whistle—**music**—cornet—light)

3. To which people did the three men belong?
   (Chaldeans—Syrians—**Jews**—Babylonians)

4. How many were thrown into the furnace?
   (1—2—**3**—4)

5. How many times hotter did the king order the
   furnace made?
   (**7**—6—2—9)

6. How many people did the king see in the furnace? (1—2—3—**4**)

7. In which Book of the Bible is this lesson written?
   (1 Kings—2 Kings—3 Samuel—**Daniel**)

Applying God's Word

1. Which words show the strong faith of Shadrach,
   Meshach, and Abednego? **(They said, "If we
   are thrown into the blazing furnace, the God
   we serve is able to save us from it. But even if
   He does not, we want you to know, O king,
   that we will not worship the image of gold.")**

2. Which character in the account may have been
   Jesus? Describe the Christlike quality of this
   character's actions. **(The fourth man in the furnace looked like the son of the gods. He
   remained with the men, protecting and sus-
   taining them in the furnace.)**

3. Why would Shadrach, Meshach, and Abednego
   still love and thank God even if He would not
   have rescued them from the furnace? **(These
   men knew blessings from God that transcend
   those of this life, including physical life
   itself.)**

50 Daniel in the Lions' Den
(Daniel 6)

Thinking about God's Word

1. Who was jealous of Daniel? **(the two other administrators)** Why did they want him out of the way? **(The king planned to set Daniel over the whole kingdom.)**

2. Why could the princes find no grounds for charges against Daniel? **(Daniel was honest and faithful.)** How did they believe they could trap him? **(by finding some way to entangle him with regards to the laws of God)**

3. What edict did they persuade the king to sign? **(Whoever prays to any god or man other than the king, would be thrown into a lions' den.)**

4. To whom did Daniel always pray? **(the true God)** How was that against the king's decree? **(According to the edict, only the king was to be worshiped.)**

5. Who reported Daniel's worship to the king? **(the administrators, advisors, and governors)**

6. How can you tell that the king thought highly of Daniel? **(He was greatly distressed when he heard of Daniel's situation and was determined to rescue him.)** Which words of the king show that Daniel must have told Darius about the God of Israel? **("May your God, whom you serve continually, rescue you!")**

7. How did Daniel say that God had protected him? **(God sent His angel, and he shut the mouths of the lions.)**

Working with God's Word

Answer each question with one word or a short phrase.

1. Which king set three administrators over his kingdom? **Darius**

2. Why could the administrators find no fault in Daniel? **Daniel was faithful to God and to his responsibilities.**

3. Who saved Daniel from the mouths of the lions? **God's angel**

4. Who was glad when he saw that Daniel was safe? **Darius**

5. To whom did Darius now want the people to pray? **the true God**

Draw a line under the answer that makes each sentence true.

1. The king made Daniel (a ruler—a king—a prince—**an administrator**) in the land.

2. No man was to pray to anyone except (God—**the king**—Daniel—the princes).

3. This law was to last for (10—3—20—**30**) days.

4. The king signed (**an edict**—a book—a petition—a dominion).

5. Daniel prayed (10—**3**—20—30) times a day.

6. Daniel was thrown into a (**den**—fiery furnace—prison—pit).

7. The king let Daniel be thrown to the lions because he (hated Daniel—**could not change the law**—wished to please the princes—wanted Daniel killed).

Applying God's Word

1. How did the desire to kill Daniel bring death upon the administrators? **(They were thrown into the lions' den after Daniel was rescued.)**

2. How did Darius now honor the God of Daniel? **(He wrote to all the people, "Reverence the God of Daniel. For He is the living God and He endures forever.")**

3. What quality of God do the words of King Darius reveal? **(God is eternal, without beginning or end.)**

51 A Message for Zechariah
(Luke 1)

Thinking about God's Word

1. Why was Gabriel sent to tell Zechariah about a son? **(so that he would know John's special role)**

2. Which words show that Gabriel came from God in answer to Zechariah's prayer? **("Your prayer has been heard.")**

3. Why did Zechariah ask, "How can I be sure of this?" **(He doubted the angel's words.)**

4. Who is "the Lord" whom John went before? **(Jesus)**

5. Name one other Bible woman who was blessed with a child only after she had become very old. **(Sarah)**

Working with God's Word

Answer each question.

1. What great event was drawing near at the time of this lesson? **the birth of Jesus, the promised Savior**

2. Which words tell that Zechariah and Elizabeth were God-fearing? **"Both of them were upright in the sight of God."**

3. Which Bible words tell that the couple was very old? **"They were both well along in years."**

4. Why was this old couple not completely happy? **They had no children**

5. What good news did an angel bring from God to Zechariah? **Elizabeth would have a son.**

6. Which words tell what great work John was to perform? **"to make ready a people prepared for the Lord"**

7. What happened to Zechariah because he doubted the promise? **He was not able to speak until the child was born.**

Answer each question correctly with one word from below.

1. Who was Zechariah's wife? **Elizabeth**

2. In which building was Zechariah burning incense? **temple**

3. What was Zechariah's child to be named? **John**

4. Like which great prophet was the child to be? **Elijah**

5. For whom was the child to prepare a way? **Jesus**

Gabriel	temple	Elizabeth
Jesus	Elijah	John
Mary	Michael	Moses

Applying God's Word

1. What is a messenger? **(one who brings news)** Why is John a messenger for Jesus? **(John told the people about Jesus' coming so that they might be ready to receive Him.)**

2. The angel came to bring Zechariah good news. How does the angel's message relate to the greatest Good News of all? **(John would come to prepare the people for the coming of the Savior of the world.)**

3. Why is it sometimes hard for us to believe what God says? **(It may not seem possible or likely to us.)**

52 The Announcement to Mary
(Luke 1; Matthew 1)

Thinking about God's Word

1. Why was Mary afraid of the angel at first? **(She was troubled and wondered what the angel's greetings meant.)**

2. With which words did Mary say that she was a servant of God? **("I am the Lord's servant.")**

3. Which words show that God, not Joseph, was to be the true Father of Jesus? **("What is conceived in her is from the Holy Spirit.")**

4. What was the Savior to be named, according to the angel's words? **(Jesus)** Find three other names for Jesus from this lesson. **(Son, Son of the Most High, Son of God)**

Working with God's Word

Answer each question.

1. What words did Gabriel use to greet Mary? **"Greetings, you who are highly favored! The Lord is with you."**

2. What was the good news the angel brought to Mary? **She was going to have a baby.**

3. In which words did Mary say that she could not understand it all? **"How will this be since I am a virgin?"**

4. In which words did the angel say that God can do everything? **"Nothing is impossible with God."**

5. How did Mary show that she believed the angel's words? **She said, "I am the Lord's servant. May it be to me as you have said."**

6. How did Joseph learn of God's wonderful promise? **in a dream**

7. How did Joseph show that he believed God's promise? **He obeyed the angel and took Mary to be his wife.**

By drawing a line from word to word, match the words given below with their meanings.

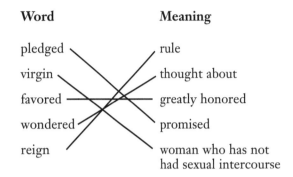

Word	Meaning
pledged	rule
virgin	thought about
favored	greatly honored
wondered	promised
reign	woman who has not had sexual intercourse

Applying God's Word

1. Which words of the lesson show that the Savior was to be true man, born of a woman? **("You will give birth to a son, and you are to give Him the name Jesus.")** What was to be His work? **("He will save His people from their sins.")**

2. Which words of the Apostles' Creed are clearly referenced in Gabriel's message to Mary? **("conceived by the Holy Spirit")**

3. Why was it necessary for the world's Savior to be a human? **(So that He might live and die in our place.)**

53 The Birth of John the Baptist
(Luke 1)

Thinking about God's Word

1. How did God's promise to Zechariah and Elizabeth come true? **(Elizabeth had a son.)**

2. Which words show that Elizabeth's neighbors and cousins knew that the child came from God? **("Her neighbors and relatives heard that the Lord had shown her great mercy.")**

3. In the naming of their son, how did the parents show that they had learned to obey and trust God without question? **(They insisted he be named John as the angel had said.)**

4. How did Zechariah use his loosed tongue, which once had spoken words of doubt at God's promise? **(to praise God and prophesy)**

Working with God's Word

Answer each question.

1. How were the angel's words fulfilled? **Zechariah spoke when the child was named.**

2. What did the parents do eight days after John was born? **circumcise him**

3. How did Zechariah settle the matter of naming the child? **He wrote, "His name is John."**

4. What did Zechariah prophesy about his son? **He would be called a prophet of the Most High, for he would go on before the Lord to prepare the way for Him to give God's people the knowledge of salvation through the forgiveness of their sins.**

5. Where was John until the day he appeared to Israel? **in the desert**

Answer each question with one word from below.

1. On which day was the baby circumcised? **eighth**

2. What did the neighbors want to name the baby? **Zechariah**

3. What did the mother name him? **John**

4. What did the father name him? **John**

5. For whom was this child to prepare the way? **Jesus**

6. Who asked for a writing tablet? **Zechariah**

7. What special ability did the Holy Spirit give Zechariah to do? **prophesy**

Zechariah	eighth	Paul	baptize
prophesy	Jesus	John	fifth

Applying God's Word

1. Which words, prophesied by Zechariah, refer to the work of Jesus, our Savior? **("He has come and has redeemed His people.")**

2. When our wisdom and learning advise us to do the opposite of what God wants, to whom must we listen? **(God)** Why? **(God knows and desires what is best for us.)**

3. How can you show your thankfulness to God for having kept His promises? **(We can thank, praise, serve, and obey Him.)**

54 The Birth of Jesus
(Luke 2)

Thinking about God's Word

1. Name three prophecies about the Savior's coming made by Old Testament prophets. **(Jesus would be born to a virgin, in Bethlehem, to a descendant of David.)**

2. Who was Caesar Augustus? **(the Roman emperor)**

3. How did God use Caesar Augustus to bring Mary and Joseph to the place where Jesus was to be born? **(Mary and Joseph had to return to Bethlehem to take part in a census ordered by Caesar.)**

4. Which simple words tell how the Savior of the world was born at Bethlehem? **("While they were there, the time came for the baby to be born, and she gave birth to her firstborn, a son. She wrapped Him in cloths and placed Him in a manger, because there was no room for them in the inn.")**

5. What difference would it make to us if Jesus had not been born? **(We would not have forgiveness, life, and salvation in His name.)**

6. How do you know that Jesus was born? **(The Bible recorded His birth.)**

7. Who gave the Christ Child to us as a gift of love? Find the answer in John 3:16. **(God)**

Working with God's Word

Answer each question.

1. What great time in the world's history now had come? **the Savior's birth**

2. What new law did the Roman emperor make for the Roman world? **The entire Roman world had to participate in a census.**

3. Who had chosen this time to fulfill His promises? **God**

4. Where was each person to go to be taxed? **to the home of their ancestors**

5. What was the name of the town to which Joseph and Mary went? **Bethlehem**

6. To whose family did Mary and Joseph belong? **David's**

7. What great happiness came to Mary in Bethlehem? **Jesus was born to her.**

8. In what did Mary wrap her baby? **cloths**

9. Who was this Child? **God's Son**

Draw a line under the word that makes each sentence true.

1. The emperor made a law that all (Romans—Jews—**the world**) should be taxed.

2. (Caesar Augustus—**Quirinius**—Julius) was the governor of Syria when Jesus was born.

3. Everyone had to go to (Rome—Bethlehem—**his own city**) to be taxed.

4. (Jerusalem—Nazareth—**Bethlehem**) was the city of David.

5. Mary laid her baby (in a cradle—on the ground—**in a manger**).

6. Mary and Joseph had come from (Syria—Jerusalem—**Nazareth**) to be taxed.

7. (David—Joseph—**God**) was the true Father of the Child Jesus.

Applying God's Word

1. Describe the circumstances surrounding the birth of the Son of God. What is unusual about the surroundings into which He was born? **(God's Son was born in humble circumstances. His mother laid Him in an animals' feedbox for His first bed.)**

2. Of what should the giving of presents at Christmas remind Christians? **(God's gift of the Savior)**

3. Why is the birth of Jesus such a significant event? **(God became a human to save us from our sins.)**

55 Angels Announce the Savior's Birth
(Luke 2)

Thinking about God's Word

1. What kind of birth announcement did God send when Jesus was born? **(Angels announced the birth to shepherds.)**

2. How did God show that He wanted the good news of His Son's birth to be known by the common, ordinary people? **(His angels brought the news to shepherds.)**

3. What was good about the news that the angel brought? **(The Savior had come.)**

4. Which words show that the good news was meant for all the people in the world? **("for all the people")**

5. What song of praise did the angels sing to God for His goodness? **("Glory to God in the highest, and on earth peace to men on whom His favor rests.")**

6. What did the shepherds do after they had heard and seen the angels? **(They went quickly to Bethlehem.)**

7. Which words show that Mary, the mother of Jesus, remembered all these events? **("Mary treasured up all these things and pondered them in her heart.")**

Working with God's Word

On the blank lines write a few words from the Bible story that answer the following questions.

1. Where were the shepherds? **in a nearby field**

2. When did the angel appear? **at night**

3. What shone around the shepherd? **the glory of the Lord**

4. Who had been born this day? **Jesus**

5. Where did the angels come from? **heaven**

6. How do you know the shepherds believed the angel? **They went immediately to see Jesus.**

7. Where did the shepherds find the baby lying? **in a manger**

Fill in the blanks with words from below.

1. The shepherds were watching over their **flocks** during the night.

2. When the angel appeared, the shepherds were **terrified**.

3. The angel called the newborn child a **Savior**.

4. A great company of the heavenly **host** sang a song of praise.

5. The shepherds spread the **word** about Jesus.

6. Mary treasured up all these things and **pondered** them in her heart.

7. The shepherds could be called the first **missionaries**.

missionaries	host	flocks	pondered
Joseph	word	Savior	terrified
Bethlehem			

Applying God's Word

1. Why is the birth of Jesus one of the all-time great events of human history? **(Jesus came to save the world from sin and its condemnation.)**

2. What is the peace that Jesus would bring? **(The peace that comes from knowing we have forgiveness, life, and salvation in Jesus.)**

3. Who told you the good news of how Jesus was born for you? **(Answers will vary.)** How can you show your thankfulness for having been told these wonderful things? **(Thank God and those who brought the Good News to you.)**

56 The Presentation of Jesus
(Luke 2)

Thinking about God's Word

1. How did Jesus' parents keep the Law of Moses for Him when He was eight days old? **(They brought Him to be circumcised.)** Which law did they obey when He was 40 days old? **(They brought Him to Jerusalem to present Him to the Lord and to offer a sacrifice.)**

2. What name was given to the Savior at the time of His circumcision? **(Jesus)** What is the meaning of that name? **(Savior)**

3. What words describing Simeon show him to be a man of faith? **(righteous and devout; the Holy Spirit was upon him)**

Working with God's Word

Answer each question.

1. Where did Jesus' parents go to present Him to the Lord? **Jerusalem**

2. Who was waiting for the Savior's coming in Jerusalem? **Simeon**

3. What special promise had been given Simeon by the Holy Spirit? **He would not die until he had seen the Lord's Christ.**

4. Why was Simeon in the temple on this day? **He was moved by the Spirit to go into the temple courts.**

5. In which words did Simeon say that the Lord had kept His promise? **"My eyes have seen Your salvation."**

6. Which of Simeon's words say that Jesus is the Savior of all people? **"A light for revelation to the Gentiles and for glory to Your people Israel."**

7. Who marveled at the words of Simeon? **Mary and Joseph**

Draw a line under the word or phrase that makes each sentence true.

1. Jesus was (born—**circumcised**—promised) on the eighth day.

2. Jesus was presented at the temple (in Nazareth—**in Jerusalem**—in Bethlehem).

3. The Holy Spirit had told Simeon that before his death he would (become very old—preach in the temple—**see the Savior**).

4. Simeon was (late and old—**righteous and devout**—very sad).

5. Simeon said that Jesus was (a great king—not a heathen—**salvation**).

Applying God's Word

1. Who is meant by the "salvation" of which Simeon spoke? **(Jesus)** How is Jesus your salvation? **(Jesus lived, died, and rose again to save me.)**

2. Why was Simeon ready to die after having seen Jesus? **(The Savior he had been waiting for had come.)**

3. Why can you die without fear, just as Simeon was able to do? **(I know Jesus is the Savior.)**

57 The Magi from the East
(Matthew 2)

Thinking about God's Word

1. Who were the people from the East who came to see Jesus? **(Magi)**

2. What led them from their land to the Holy Land? **(a star)** Why did they need a star to guide them? **(They didn't know where the Savior was.)**

3. How did the chief priests and scribes of Jesus' time discover where the Savior was to be born? See Micah 5:2 in your Bible. **(They studied the Old Testament prophecies.)**

4. Who said to the Magi, "Go and make a careful search for the child"? **(Herod)**

5. Why did Herod ask the Magi to let him know where Jesus was to be found? **(He wanted to kill the newborn King.)** Why did God warn the Magi not to tell Herod where Jesus was? **(God wanted to prevent Herod from killing Jesus.)**

Working with God's Word

Answer each question.

1. What are the Magi also called? **Wise Men**

2. Why was Herod disturbed at the words of the Magi? **He was the king of the Jews.**

3. From whom did Herod learn where Jesus was to be born? **the chief priests and teachers of the law**

4. What answer was given Herod when he wished to know Jesus' birthplace? **Bethlehem, in the land of Judah**

5. How did the Magi show that they believed Jesus to be God? **They bowed down and worshiped Him.**

Answer each question with words from below.

1. From where did the Wise Men come? **East**

2. At which city did they stop for information? **Jerusalem**

3. What did the Wise Men call Jesus? **King of the Jews**

4. Who was troubled about the Wise Men's question? **Herod**

5. What led the Wise Men from the East? **star**

6. Whom did the Wise Men find with the Child? **Mary**

7. How did God warn the Magi not to see Herod? **by a dream**

Mary	aloes	Jerusalem
Nazareth	East	by an angel
by a dream	Herod	King of the Jews
Persia	star	

Applying God's Word

1. What did Herod not understand about Jesus' kingship? See Jesus' words to Pilate in John 18:33–37. **(Jesus is not a king in the political use of the term. Rather Jesus is the ruler of the universe, the Lord of all who love and trust in Him.)**

2. How were the words of Simeon being fulfilled at the coming of the Magi? See Luke 2:32. **(Simeon prophesied that Jesus would be "a light for revelation to the Gentiles." The Magi were Gentiles who came to Jesus from another land.)**

3. What action on the part of the Magi suggests that they believed in Jesus as the Savior (Matthew 2:11)? **(They worshiped Him and offered Him gifts—gold, frankincense, and myrrh.)**

58 The Escape to Egypt
(Matthew 2)

Thinking about God's Word

1. Jeremiah prophesied the "Slaughter of the Innocents," which took place at this time. In what respect were the boys in Bethlehem innocent? **(They were not executed for any crime they committed.)**

2. How might one of the gifts that the Magi brought to Jesus have been put to good use at this time? **(They could use the gold to help pay travel expenses.)**

3. Why should God's children be happy to know that the angels are always near them? **(Angels are God's helpers and representatives.)** How did God use angels in this story? **(They brought messages from God to Joseph.)**

4. Name other Bible people who lived in Egypt. **(Answers will vary.)**

5. By whom were the ancestors of Jesus led out of Egypt? **(Moses)**

Working with God's Word

Fill in the blanks.

1. The angel of the Lord appeared to **Joseph** in a dream.

2. Herod was seeking the young Child to **kill** Him.

3. Joseph traveled with the young Child and the mother during the **night**.

4. Herod killed boys **two** years old and under.

5. An angel of the Lord appeared in a dream to Joseph in **Egypt**.

6. Joseph was told to take Mary and Jesus back to the land of **Israel**.

7. They returned and lived in a city called **Nazareth**.

Applying God's Word

1. What details of this account show Joseph to be a man of faith? How do others come to know about your faith in Jesus? **(Joseph obeyed the word of the Lord. Others come to know of our faith, not only through our words, but also through our actions.)**

2. What does it mean to you to know that God kept all His promises and prophecies in Jesus? **(We are saved and forgiven.)**

3. How did God defend Jesus against all danger and guard and protect Him from all evil? **(He told Joseph to take Mary and Jesus to Egypt.)** How does God do the same for you daily? **(He guards and protects us from evil.)**

59 The Boy Jesus at the Temple
(Luke 2)

Thinking about God's Word

1. When Jesus was 12 years old, where did His parents take Him? **(Jerusalem)**

2. Which words tell that Jesus' parents were faithful worshipers at the temple? **(They went to Jerusalem every year.)**

3. Where did Jesus say He had been while His parents looked for Him? **(in His Father's house)**

4. Read Colossians 2:3. How did the teachers in the temple find the words to be true? **(The teachers in the temple were amazed at His understanding and answers.)**

5. Why did Jesus study Scripture even though "all the treasures of wisdom and knowledge" are to be found in Him? **(According to His human nature, He grew in knowledge through the study of God's Word.)**

6. Which words tell that Mary and Joseph were very worried over the thought of losing Jesus? **("Your father and I have been anxiously searching for You.")**

7. What reason did Jesus give for staying behind in Jerusalem? **(He had to be in His Father's house.)**

Working with God's Word

Answer each question.

1. What great festival did Jesus' parents attend each year? **Passover**

2. Where was this festival held? **Jerusalem**

3. Why did the parents not worry over Jesus' absence on the return trip? **They thought he was traveling with relatives and friends.**

4. How long did Joseph and Mary look for Jesus before finding Him? **three days**

5. What was it about Jesus that amazed all who heard Him? **His understanding and His answers**

6. In which words did Jesus answer the question His mother asked Him? **"Didn't you know I had to be in My Father's house?"**

7. What was His Father's house? **the temple**

On the blank lines write the word from below that you think of as you read each sentence.

1. It lasted seven days. **Passover**

2. Jesus was sitting in the midst of them. **teachers**

3. Where they found Jesus. **temple**

4. Jesus had to be about His business. **His Father's**

5. Mary, Joseph, and Jesus returned there to live. **Nazareth**

6. Here it was that Mary kept all Jesus' sayings. **heart**

7. Jesus kept this commandment when He obeyed His parents. **fourth**

temple	fourth	heart
Passover	first	teachers
Nazareth	His Father's	

Applying God's Word

1. What details of this account show Jesus to be true God? What details of this account show Jesus to be truly human? **(Jesus showed Himself to be about the business of His Father in heaven. Jesus was obedient also to His earthly parents. He grew and learned as other children do.)**

2. What has been offered to you to help you in learning and knowing Scripture? Name people and things that have helped you. **(Answers will vary.)**

3. Two commandments of God were clearly obeyed by Jesus in this lesson. What are they? How did Jesus obey them? How can you follow His example? **(The Third Commandment and the Fourth Commandment. Jesus studied God's Word, and He was obedient to His heavenly Father and His parents. We, too, can worship God and obey God and our parents.)**

60 The Baptism of Jesus
(Matthew 3; Mark 1)

Thinking about God's Word

1. Who came to John to be baptized? **(Jesus)**

2. How can you tell that John recognized Jesus as the Christ? **(John said, "I need to be baptized by You, and do You come to me?")**

3. What was the theme of the message John preached? **(repentance)**

4. How did God show Jesus as the Savior whom He had promised to send? **(He said, "You are My Son, whom I love; with You I am well pleased.")**

5. What prophet foretold the ministry of John the Baptist? **(Isaiah)**

Working with God's Word

Answer each question.

1. How did John answer Jesus when He asked to be baptized? **"I need to be baptized by You, and do You come to me?"**

2. What reason did Jesus give John for being baptized by him? **Jesus said, "Let it be so now; it is proper for us to do this to fulfill all righteousness."**

3. How was each person of the Trinity shown at this baptism? **Jesus was baptized, the Father spoke, and the Spirit descended like a dove.**

On the blank lines write words from below.

1. He came from Galilee to the Jordan. **Jesus**

2. He preached in the desert. **John**

3. He descended like a dove. **Holy Spirit**

4. He said, "I need to be baptized by You." **John**

5. He said, "Let it be so now." **Jesus**

6. He is the Father's beloved Son. **Jesus**

7. Who wrote the first book of the New Testament? **Matthew**

| Holy Spirit | God the Father | John |
| Matthew | John the Baptist | Jesus |

Applying God's Word

1. In what way did John "prepare the way for the Lord"? **(John told the people to repent for the kingdom of God was near.)**

2. In what two ways did the people respond to the preaching of John? **(People confessed their sins and were baptized by John.)**

3. Why did Jesus not need to be baptized as a sign of repentance? **(Jesus committed no sin and therefore had no need to repent.)** Why, then, was He baptized? **(He was baptized because He was obedient to God in our place.)**

61 The Temptation of Jesus
(Matthew 4)

Thinking about God's Word

1. Into whose power had man fallen when Adam sinned? **(Satan's)**

2. Why had Jesus come into the world? **(to save fallen humanity)**

3. Why did Satan want to keep Jesus from doing His work? **(All humanity would remain in his control if Jesus failed.)** How did the devil plan to spoil what Jesus had come to do? **(He wanted to entice Jesus to sin.)**

4. How did the devil first try to plant the seed of doubt into Jesus, as he once had done to Adam and Eve? **(He said, "If You are the Son of God.")**

5. When Satan tempted Jesus the second time, how did he try to twist God's Word to lead Jesus into sin? **(He told Jesus to throw Himself off the temple because God has promised in His Word that the holy angels will protect God's people.)** How had he twisted God's Word in the Garden of Eden? **(He asked Eve if God really said they weren't to eat from any tree of the garden, twisting what God actually said.)**

6. In the third temptation, how did the devil use humankind's love for honor and possessions to try to lead the Savior into sin? **(He showed Jesus all the kingdoms and splendor of the world, promising them to Jesus if Jesus would worship him.)** How had he used the same kind of temptation against Adam and Eve? **(He led Adam and Eve to believe that they could be like God.)**

7. Which words spoken three times show that Jesus knew Scripture and used it correctly against the devil? **("It is written.")**

Working with God's Word

Answer each question.

1. Where was Jesus led after His baptism? **into the desert**

2. How long did Jesus fast there? **40 days and 40 nights**

3. In which words did the devil first tempt Jesus to sin? **"If You are the Son of God, tell these stones to become bread."**

4. According to Jesus' words, by what shall man really live? **"every word that comes from the mouth of God"**

5. Where did the devil take Jesus for the second temptation? **to the highest point of the temple**

6. How did the devil tempt Jesus there? **He said, "Throw Yourself down. For it is written: 'He will command His angels concerning you, and they will lift you up in their hands, so that you will not strike your foot against a stone.' "**

7. In which words did Jesus answer this temptation? **"It is also written: 'Do not put the Lord your God to the test.' "**

8. What did the devil say in tempting Jesus the third time? **"All this I will give You if You will bow down and worship me."**

9. What was Jesus' final answer to the devil's temptations? **"Away from Me, Satan! For it is written: 'Worship the Lord your God, and serve Him only.' "**

Fill in the blanks with words from below.

1. Jesus said, "Away from Me, **Satan**."

2. The devil asked Jesus to turn **stones** to bread.

3. The devil showed Jesus all the **kingdoms** of the world.

4. Angels came and **attended** Jesus.

5. Jesus was led into the wilderness by the **Spirit**.

6. The devil asked Jesus to fall down and **worship** him.

7. Jesus said, "Do not put the **Lord** your God to the test."

8. The devil had Jesus stand on the **highest** point of the temple.

9. Three times Jesus said, "It is **written**."

written	kingdoms	Satan	worship
attended	Lord	Spirit	highest
stones			

Applying God's Word

1. What was the difference in outcome between Satan's attempt to lead Adam into sin and his attempt to lead Jesus into sin? **(Adam fell into sin; Jesus resisted temptation.)**

2. This account shows how Jesus obeyed God's Law in our place. Explain. **(Jesus resisted temptation in our place. The devil was unable to entice Jesus to sin.)**

3. In facing and resisting temptation, Jesus pointed us to the means through which the Holy Spirit strengthens us to resist temptations. What is that means? **(Jesus resisted the devil through His use of the Word of God. Through the same Word of God the Holy Spirit strengthens and encourages us for the new life He has called us to live in Him.)**

62 Jesus Helps Peter Catch Fish
(Luke 5)

Thinking about God's Word

1. Show that the people in this story were eager to hear God's Word. **(People were crowding around Jesus.)**

2. What do you think Jesus talked about to the people? **(people's sin and God's love, grace, and forgiveness)**

3. Why did Simon not seem to think it wise to go fishing again? **(They had fished all night and caught nothing.)** What was it that made him willing to let down the net, nevertheless? **(Jesus' command)**

4. Which words show that the nets had not been made to hold so great a number of fish? **("Their nets began to break.")**

5. Which words show that the two boats together had not been built large enough to hold the catch of fish that Jesus gave them? **("They began to sink.")**

6. How did Peter show that he knew he had seen a miracle? **("He fell at Jesus' knees and said, 'Go away from me, Lord; I am a sinful man!' ")**

7. Which words say that these disciples now gave their whole life to become followers and disciples of Jesus? **("So they pulled their boats up on shore, left everything and followed Him.")**

Working with God's Word

Answer each question on the blank line.

1. Why do you think Jesus got on a boat to teach the people? **The people were crowding around Him.**

2. Whose ship did Jesus use? **Simon's**

3. What was Jesus' command to Simon after He had finished speaking? **"Put out into deep water, and let down the nets for a catch."**

4. Which words tell why Simon was willing to let down the nets? **"because You say so"**

5. Which words tell that many fish were in the net? **"They caught such a large number of fish that their nets began to break."**

6. What did Simon Peter say when he saw all the fish? **"Go away from me, Lord; I am a sinful man!"**

7. How did these disciples give themselves to Jesus from then on? **They left everything and followed Him.**

Draw a line under the correct answer to each question.

1. What is another name for the Sea of Galilee? (Red Sea—Salt Sea—**Lake of Gennesaret**—Dead Sea)

2. How was the water where Jesus told the disciples to fish? (**deep**—shallow—muddy—warm)

3. How many fish did they catch? (none—1—a few—**many**)

4. What did Jesus tell Simon Peter that he would catch from now on? (fish—draughts—thieves—**men**)

5. How many boats were filled with fish? (1—**2**—3—4—5—6—none—many)

Applying God's Word

1. Why did Jesus teach and preach? **(to free the people from their sins)** What did He preach about? **(human sin and God's grace and forgiveness)**

2. By what action did Peter demonstrate his faith in Jesus? **(Peter obeyed Jesus, letting down the nets even after they had fished and caught nothing all night.)** By what words? **(Peter said, "Go away from me, Lord; I am a sinful man!")**

3. What does the amount of fish in the catch show about the growth expected in God's kingdom? **(Just as Peter and the other disciples caught a large catch of fish at Jesus' command, Peter and the other apostles later brought large numbers of people into God's kingdom as the Holy Spirit worked through their preaching.)**

63 Jesus Changes Water to Wine
(John 2)

Thinking about God's Word

1. Why was it not hard for Jesus' followers to believe that He was a true man? **(He was born into a human family and did things with other people such as attend weddings.)**

2. How did Jesus show Himself to be true God before the people at Cana? **(He turned water into wine.)**

3. What did Jesus use to turn water into wine? **(only the power of His word)**

4. Which words of the lesson tell why He did this miracle? **("He thus revealed His glory, and His disciples put their faith in Him.")**

5. Who went to Jesus for help in this lesson? **(Jesus' mother)** Why should we go to Jesus when we need help? **(He is the only real source of help.)**

6. No doubt John was present at Cana when Jesus did His first miracle. How did John and the other disciples see the glory of Jesus at Cana? **(They witnessed Jesus' first miracle.)**

7. How many gallons did each water jar hold? **(20 to 30)** How many jars were there? **(6)**

Working with God's Word

Answer the questions.

1. What trouble brought Mary to Jesus for His help? **The wine was gone.**

2. Why were six water jars in the house? **They were used for ceremonial washing.**

3. To whom was some water taken after it had been changed to wine? **the master of the banquet**

4. Which words tell where Jesus began doing miracles? **"at Cana in Galilee"**

5. Which words tell why Jesus did this great miracle? **"He thus revealed His glory, and His disciples put their faith in Him."**

Fill in the blanks with words from below.

1. There was a wedding in the city of **Cana**.

2. Mary, Jesus, and His **disciples** were invited.

3. The people ran out of **wine**.

4. Jesus said, "My **time** has not yet come."

5. Mary told the **servants** to do whatever Jesus might command.

6. There were **six** stone water jars in this home.

7. The servants filled the water jars to the **brim**.

8. By His power, Jesus turned the **water** into good wine.

servants	mother	time
six	eight	wine
Cana	miracles	brim
water	disciples	father

Applying God's Word

1. How do we know that Mary had faith in Jesus' power? **(Mary told the servants, "Do whatever He tells you.")**

2. Tell how this account shows Jesus as both true man and true God. **(As true man, Jesus went to celebrate at a wedding with His disciples. As true God, Jesus performed a miracle, changing water into wine.)**

3. What does this account indicate about the scope of human problems about which Jesus is concerned? **(Jesus is concerned about all the things that trouble, inconvenience, embarrass, or threaten to harm us.)**

64 Jesus Calms the Storm
(Mark 4)

Thinking about God's Word

1. How can it be shown from this lesson that Jesus was true man? **(He fell asleep.)**

2. Why did the disciples awaken Jesus? **(They feared they would drown and asked Jesus to save them.)**

3. Why did they ask Jesus for His help even though they were experienced sailors? **(The boat was nearly swamped by the waves.)**

4. How did Jesus still the storm? **(He said, "Quiet! Be still!")**

5. Why did the wind and sea obey Jesus? **(He controls them.)**

6. Show from this lesson that Jesus was true God-man. **(Although He slept like a normal man, Jesus demonstrated His power over the wind and waves.)**

7. Who permitted this great storm to come up? **(God)** Why does God let trials and temptations come to His children? **(to test our faith and demonstrate His power and glory)**

Working with God's Word

Circle T for true and F for false.

1. This lesson says: "It had been a busy day for Jesus." T **F**

2. This lesson says: "Jesus was tired from a hard day's work." T **F**

3. This lesson says: "They got into a boat and set out." **T** F

4. This lesson says: "As they sailed, He fell asleep." **T** F

5. This lesson says: "A furious squall came up." **T** F

6. This lesson says: "And His disciples came to Him." T **F**

7. This lesson says: "Lord, save us!" **T** F

8. This lesson says: "Why are you so afraid?" **T** F

9. This lesson says: "He arose and quieted the wind." T **F**

10. This lesson says: "Then the wind died down and it was completely calm." **T** F

Circle Yes or No.

1. Jesus and His disciples wanted to reach the other side of the lake. **Yes** No

2. Because Jesus slept, we know that He was true God. Yes **No**

3. The great storm awakened Jesus. Yes **No**

4. Jesus asked the disciples why they had no faith. **Yes** No

5. Jesus said to the sea, "Quiet! Be still!" **Yes** No

Applying God's Word

1. Which part of the disciples' cry showed that they were without trust and hope, even while they asked Jesus for help? **(They said, "Lord, save us! We're going to drown!")** Why was this wrong? **(The disciples failed to place their trust in Jesus.)**

2. In which words did Jesus tell the disciples what the real reason for all their worry and fear had been? **(Jesus said, "Why are you so afraid? Do you still have no faith?")**

3. Why can we always trust in Jesus? **(Jesus is always with us.)**

112

65 Jesus Heals a Man Who Was Paralyzed

(Mark 2)

Thinking about God's Word

1. Why did the four men bring their sick friend to Jesus? **(Their friend was troubled because of his sins.)** How did they show their faith in His power to help? **(They made an opening in the roof of the house and lowered their friend to Jesus.)**

2. Which words tell what the man needed more than the healing of his body? **("Son, your sins are forgiven.")** How could Jesus know this about the man? **(As God, Jesus knows all things.)**

3. Why did the teachers think that Jesus had mocked God? **(Jesus forgave the man of his sins, something only God can do.)**

4. What do we learn from the fact that Jesus could tell their thoughts? **(Jesus knows all things.)**

5. How did Jesus prove His power? **(He healed the man of his paralysis.)**

Working with God's Word

Answer each question with one word or a short phrase.

1. What was the sickness that the man of this lesson had? **paralysis**

2. To which city did the Lord return? **Capernaum**

3. How many men carried the sick man? **four**

4. What did the men do so the man could reach Jesus? **took apart the roof and lowered the man to Jesus**

5. What did Jesus call the sick man when He spoke to him? **Son**

Draw a line under the word or phrase that makes each sentence true.

1. Jesus was (outside—**inside**) when the man was brought to Him.

2. The first thing Jesus did for the man was to (ask his name—heal his sickness—**forgive his sins**).

3. (Jesus—The sick man—**The teachers**) said, "Who can forgive sins but God alone?"

4. Jesus called Himself (the Messiah—**the Son of Man**—the Just One) in this lesson.

5. The teachers spoke evil things of Jesus (**to themselves**—so that all could hear it—in a low voice).

6. Jesus told the sick man to take up his (blanket—couch—mattress—**mat**) and go home.

7. The people who saw this miracle (laughed at the scribes—told Jesus to leave their country—**glorified God**).

Applying God's Word

1. Describe the kind of friends God provided the man with paralysis. **(The man's friends went through great effort to bring the man to Jesus.)**

2. Which words of the lesson show why Jesus did miracles openly? **("But that you may know that the Son of Man has authority on earth to forgive sins.")**

3. According to this account, what type of healing provided by Jesus do people need the most? **(forgiveness of sins)**

66 A Widow's Son and Jairus' Daughter

(Luke 7–8)

Thinking about God's Word

1. How did Jesus raise the widow's son to life? **(He simply told the young man to get up.)**

2. Why was Jairus wise in going to Jesus for help? **(Jesus is the only true source of help in life's struggles and difficulties.)**

3. What did Jesus mean when He said, "The girl is not dead but asleep"? **(He could bring the girl to life as simply as if He were wakening her from sleep.)**

4. At what other time did Jesus prove that He had the same power? **(when He rose from the dead)**

5. Why did Jesus' words "Don't cry," as spoken to the widow, have comfort and meaning for her? **(He brought her son back to life.)**

Working with God's Word

Answer each question.

1. What did Jesus meet as He entered Nain one day? **a funeral procession**

2. How did Jesus show His great sorrow for the mother? **He told her not to cry and brought her son back to life.**

3. By which miracle did Jesus comfort the mother? **He brought her son back to life.**

4. In which words did the people glorify God upon seeing the miracle? **"They were all filled with awe and praised God."**

5. How did Jairus show his faith in Jesus? **He pleaded with Jesus to come to his house because his daughter was dying.**

6. What sad message did someone bring to Jairus? **"Your daughter is dead."**

7. How did Jesus show the people His power over death? **He brought the girl back to life.**

Draw a line under the correct answer to each question.

1. How many sons did the widow have? (**1**—2—3—4—0—5)

2. On what was the young man being carried? (bed—stretcher—**coffin**—bier)

3. Over what was Jairus a ruler? (Palestine—**synagogue**—Judea—Galilee)

4. How old was his sick daughter? (30—**12**—20—5—6)

5. What did Jesus call death in this lesson? (the end of everything—damnation—**sleep**—heaven)

6. How did the people in Jairus' house show unbelief in Jesus? (cast Him out—**laughed at Him**—left the room—closed their ears)

7. What was given Jairus' daughter after Jesus brought her to life? (**food**—wine—water—rest)

Applying God's Word

1. How did Jesus show the people of Jairus' city His power over death? **(He brought the young girl back to life.)**

2. Because of Jesus, the death of Jairus' daughter and of the widow's son really was just a short sleep that had a happy ending. Why does death mean the same thing for you too? **(Jesus has promised to raise from the dead all who believe in Him.)**

3. Responding to the restoration of the young man of Nain, the people said, "God has come to help His people." Describe the help Jesus came to provide. **(Jesus came to bring forgiveness, new life, and salvation to all people. Physical life endures for a time; these blessings last forever.)**

67 Jesus Feeds More Than Five Thousand

(John 6)

Thinking about God's Word

1. What did Jesus ask Philip? **("Where shall we buy bread for these people to eat?")** How did Philip's answer show that he thought money was of first importance in getting food for hungry people? **(He said, "Eight months' wages would not buy enough bread for each one to have a bite!")**

2. Why was Andrew's answer a hopeless response to Jesus' question? **(Five small barley loaves and two small fish could never feed 5,000 people.)**

3. In which prayer do we say, "Give us this day our daily bread"? **(Lord's Prayer)** Why do we ask for it even when we know we'll get it? **(So that we remember that all we have comes from the hand of our gracious God.)**

Working with God's Word

Fill in the blanks.

1. A great **crowd** followed Jesus.

2. Jesus went up on a **mountainside**.

3. When Jesus looked up, He saw a great **crowd**.

4. Jesus said to **Philip**, "Where shall we buy bread?"

5. **Andrew** found the boy with loaves and fishes.

6. Before Jesus gave out food, He **thanked** God.

7. He distributed to the people as much food as they **wanted**.

8. Twelve baskets were filled with the **food** that remained.

9. The people saw that Jesus had done a **miracle**.

Mark the true sentences T and the false sentences F.

1. **T** Jesus crossed to the far side of the Sea of Galilee.

2. **F** Jesus asked Andrew, "Where shall we buy bread?"

3. **T** Philip said that eight months' wages would not be enough.

4. **T** Andrew found a boy who had a little food with him.

5. **T** The boy had two fishes and five barley loaves.

6. **F** Jesus gave each of the five thousand a loaf and a fish.

7. **T** The people ate as much as they wanted.

Applying God's Word

1. Jesus' miracles led the people to see Jesus as a great prophet. Jesus is more than a prophet. Explain. **(Jesus is the very Son of God and Savior of the world.)**

2. Which words of the lesson show that Jesus gave the people more than they wanted and needed? **(They filled 12 baskets with leftovers.)** Why could He do this? **(Jesus is God.)**

3. Jesus could have simply taken away the people's hunger. Instead, He satisfied their hunger by multiplying a meager lunch of bread and fish. In another meal, the Lord's Supper, Jesus also provides for His followers. What do they receive with the bread and wine? **(With the bread and wine recipients receive the very body and blood of Christ.)** What benefits are received? **(They receive forgiveness of sins, new life, and salvation.)**

68 Jesus Walks on the Water
(Mark 6; Matthew 14)

Thinking about God's Word

1. What did the multitude whom Jesus fed want to do to Him? **(make Him king by force)**

2. How did the disciples obey Jesus' command? **(They got into a boat and left for Capernaum.)** How was their faith tested that night? **(They were terrified at the sight of Jesus walking on the lake.)**

3. How did they show that they didn't believe that it was Jesus when they saw Him coming toward them? **(They said, "It's a ghost.")**

4. What did Jesus say to them? **("Take courage! It is I. Don't be afraid.")** How did those words show why He had come to them? **(He had come to be with them, to comfort them with His peace.)**

5. Why could Jesus walk on water? **(Jesus is God; He can do anything.)** Why could Peter walk on water? **(Jesus gave him the power to walk on water.)**

6. What did Peter cry out when he began to sink? **(He recognized his need for help from Jesus.)**

7. Which words of Jesus tell why Peter began to sink? **("You of little faith.")** How did Jesus show Peter that He was the merciful Son of God? **(He reached out and caught Peter, rescuing him.)**

Working with God's Word

Answer each question with one word from the story.

1. Whom did Jesus send away? **crowd**

2. Who went before Him to Bethsaida? **disciples**

3. During which watch did Jesus come to His disciples? **fourth**

4. What did the disciples think Jesus was when they saw Him? **ghost**

5. With which word did Jesus tell Peter to come to Him? **"Come"**

6. How did Peter become when he saw the wind blowing? **afraid**

7. What died down when Jesus stepped into the boat? **wind**

Draw a line under the correct answer to each question.

1. Whom did the people want for their king? (Herod—Tabors—**Jesus**—Philip)

2. Why did Jesus go up on a mountainside? (to preach—**to pray**—to hide—to rest)

3. Where was the boat when a storm arose? **(a distance from land**—on the other side—along the coast)

4. How did Jesus cross the sea to get to the disciples? (by rowing—by sailing—by swimming—**by walking**)

5. What happened when Jesus climbed into the boat? (The disciples cried—The disciples rowed to shore—**The wind died down)**

Applying God's Word

1. Jesus spoke to His disciples in their fear, saying, "Take courage! It is I. Don't be afraid." How do these words of Jesus apply also to us? **(Jesus similarly invites us to trust in Him. We also need not be afraid.)**

2. What happened when Peter trusted in Jesus? What happened when he doubted? **(When Peter trusted in Jesus, he was able to walk on the water; when Peter doubted, he began to sink.)**

3. What realization led the disciples to worship Jesus? **(The disciples worshiped Jesus, saying, "Truly You are the Son of God.")**

69 The Faith of a Canaanite Woman
(Matthew 15)

Thinking about God's Word

1. What made it seem that Jesus did not care to help the Canaanite woman? **(At first Jesus did not answer her. Then He commented that He had been sent to the lost sheep of Israel.)**

2. For what reason did the disciples ask Jesus to send her away? **(She kept crying out after them.)**

3. Why did Jesus say that the woman had no right to ask for His help? **(Jesus said He had come for Israel.)**

4. In which words did the woman answer Jesus when He said that helping her would be like throwing children's bread to dogs? **("Even the dogs eat the crumbs that fall from their masters' table.")**

5. In which words did Jesus say why He would answer the woman's prayer? **("Woman, you have great faith! Your request is granted.")**

Working with God's Word

Answer each question.

1. Who came to Jesus for help? **a Canaanite woman**

2. With which words did the woman tell what was wrong with her daughter? **"My daughter is suffering terribly from demon-possession."**

3. Who said, "Send her away, for she keeps crying out after us"? **Jesus' disciples**

4. Which words say that Jesus came for the Jews first? **"I was sent only to the lost sheep of Israel."**

5. With which words did the woman worship Jesus? **"Lord, Son of David, have mercy on me!"**

6. In which words did Jesus praise this woman's faith? **"Woman, you have great faith!"**

7. How did Jesus answer the faithful prayer of this woman? **He healed her daughter.**

Draw a line under the answer that makes each sentence true.

1. The woman who came to Jesus was a (Jew— Roman—**Greek**—Galilean—Babylonian).

2. The woman asked for (bread—**mercy**—meat— alms—great riches).

3. At first Jesus answered the woman (**not a word**—"Go to a doctor"—"Depart from Me"— very kindly).

4. Jesus told the woman that her (daughter's sickness—sin—**faith**—age) was great.

5. Her daughter was healed from that (year—day— **hour**).

Applying God's Word

1. Which words of the woman showed that she knew Jesus to be the promised Savior? **("Lord, Son of David")**

2. Which words show that the woman knew she didn't deserve the help she was asking of Him? **("But even the dogs eat the crumbs that fall from their masters' table.")**

3. In what way is each of us like the woman in the lesson? What does the lesson teach us about Jesus? **(Each of us is unworthy of the salvation Jesus freely offers us. Jesus loves and desires to save all people.)**

70 The Ten Lepers
(Luke 17)

Thinking about God's Word

1. Where was Jesus going? **(Jerusalem)**

2. Why did the men want Jesus to have pity on them? **(They had leprosy.)**

3. Who came back to praise God? **(one leper, a Samaritan)**

4. What did Jesus mean when He said, "Where are the other nine?" **(Why didn't the others also return to offer their thanks and praise?)**

5. Why was the leper healed? **(He had faith in Jesus.)**

Working with God's Word

Fill in the blank with a word from the story.

1. Jesus traveled along the border between **Samaria** and Galilee.

2. **Ten** men with leprosy met Him.

3. They called, "Jesus, **Master**, have pity on us!"

4. Jesus told them to show themselves to the **priests**.

5. One of the men came back and **praised** God in a loud voice.

6. Jesus asked, "Were not all ten **cleansed**?"

7. "Where are the other **nine**?"

8. Jesus said to the Samaritan, "**Rise** and go; your faith has made you well."

Write who made these statements. Use the words Jesus *or* 10 men.

1. "Were not all ten cleansed?" **Jesus**

2. "Rise and go; your faith has made you well." **Jesus**

3. "Jesus, Master, have pity on us." **10 men**

4. "Was no one found to return and give praise to God except this foreigner?" **Jesus**

5. "Where are the other nine?" **Jesus**

6. "Go, show yourselves to the priests." **Jesus**

Applying God's Word

1. Why did Jesus want the men to see the priests? **(Jesus had healed them of their leprosy. The priests would verify that they were healed.)**

2. Tell how this account shows Jesus as the Lord and Savior of all people. **(Jesus demonstrated His desire to help and save those who were looked down on by society, including lepers and Samaritans.)**

3. What example does the Samaritan provide for all of us who love and trust in Jesus as our Savior? **(The Samaritan thanked and praised the Savior for helping him.)**

71 Jesus Blesses the Children
(Matthew 18–19)

Thinking about God's Word

1. What did the disciples ask Jesus? **("Who is the greatest in the kingdom of heaven?")**

2. With which direct words did Jesus tell them that if they didn't change, they wouldn't get into the kingdom of heaven? **("I tell you the truth, unless you change and become like little children, you will never enter the kingdom of heaven.")**

3. How did Jesus warn the disciples that they were not to look lightly upon the child who stood in their midst nor to offend such a little believer? **(He said, "But if anyone causes one of these little ones who believe in Me to sin, it would be better for him to have a large millstone hung around his neck and to be drowned in the depths of the sea.")**

4. In which words did Jesus tell the disciples that they were to lead little children to Him rather than to keep them away? **("Let the little children come to Me, and do not hinder them, for the kingdom of God belongs to such as these.")**

5. Who did Jesus say is the greatest in His kingdom? **(whoever humbles himself like a child)**

Working with God's Word

Answer each question.

1. To whom is Jesus a particular friend? **children**

2. Whom did Jesus call the greatest in the kingdom of heaven? **whoever humbles himself like a child**

3. Whom do people welcome when they welcome a child in Jesus' name? **Jesus**

4. Which words tell that the disciples scolded those who brought them? **"But the disciples rebuked those who brought them."**

5. In which words did Jesus say that He wanted children to come to Him? **"Let the children come to Me, and do not hinder them."**

Draw a line under the correct answer to each question.

1. Who came to Jesus to ask Him a question? (parents—**disciples**—children—scribes)

2. What did they want to know? (Who Jesus' best friend was—If He loved children—**Who would be greatest in the kingdom of heaven**)

3. How can a person become as a little child? (by not studying too much—**by trusting altogether in Jesus**—by not sinning)

4. When is a child not a child of God? (when the child does not go to church every Sunday—when the child becomes older—**when the child does not believe**)

5. Why were the children brought to Jesus? (for Him to heal them—for Him to teach them—**for Him to pray for them**)

6. How did Jesus feel when He saw what the disciples did? (He wept—**He was not pleased**—He was pleased)

7. How did Jesus show His love for the little ones? (He gave them presents—He kissed them—He preached to them—**He blessed them**)

Applying God's Word

1. Why must little children simply trust their parents for everything they need? **(They lack the ability to provide for themselves.)** With which words did Jesus tell the disciples that in order to be in His kingdom they must be toward Him as little children are toward parents? **("I tell you the truth, unless you change and become like little children, you will never enter the kingdom of heaven.")**

2. According to this account, how does God in heaven protect little children? **(God sends angels to protect them.)**

3. How do people "change and become like little children" in order to enter the kingdom of heaven? **(The Holy Spirit changes people's hearts, creating childlike, trusting faith through God's Word.)**

72 The Transfiguration
(Matthew 17)

Thinking about God's Word

1. What did Jesus look like in His transfiguration? **(His face shone like the sun, and His clothes became white as light.)**

2. Who appeared with Jesus? **(Moses and Elijah)**

3. Which disciples went with Jesus up the mountain? **(Peter, James, and John)**

4. What did Peter want to do for Jesus? **(Peter wanted to put up three shelters, one for Jesus, one for Moses, and one for Elijah.)**

5. What did the voice from the cloud say? **("This is My Son whom I love; with Him I am well pleased. Listen to Him!")**

6. Why were the disciples afraid? **(They heard the voice of God.)**

7. Why did Jesus tell them not to tell anyone what they had seen? **(This experience was to be shared after Jesus had risen from the dead.)**

Working with God's Word

Write T for true or F for false.

1. Jesus took Peter, James, and Matthew with Him to the mountain. **False**

2. Jesus was transfigured on the mountain. **True**

3. Elijah and Isaiah appeared, talking with Jesus. **False**

4. The men were talking about Jesus' departure. **True**

5. The disciples were sleepy. **True**

6. Peter offered to build three shelters. **True**

7. God's voice came from a fire. **False**

8. The disciples were terrified of the voice. **True**

Fill in the blanks with words from below.

After **six** days Jesus took **Peter**, **James**, and John up a mountain. He was **transfigured** before them. Two men, **Moses** and **Elijah**, appeared with Jesus. Peter offered to build **shelters** for the three. A voice came from a **cloud** saying Jesus was God's **Son**. **Jesus** told the disciples not to tell what they had seen.

Moses	two	Peter
cloud	Jesus	six
John	transfigured	Elijah
Son	James	shelters

Applying God's Word

1. What theme from the life and teaching of the prophets was fulfilled in Christ? **(Moses and Elijah both prophesied about the coming Savior of the world.)**

2. What event, about to take place in Jerusalem, became the subject of those talking with Jesus at His transfiguration? **(Moses and Elijah talked with Jesus about His coming sacrifice in Jerusalem for the sins of the world.)** Why was this topic significant? **(This event was long anticipated by God's Old Testament people.)**

3. Tell the meaning of the words spoken from the bright cloud for the disciples and for you. **(God identified Jesus as His Son. Those witnessing the event saw Jesus in His glory and recognized Him as the promised Messiah. God tells all followers of all time to listen to Jesus. We have His words written for us in God's Word. We, too, are to listen to His Word.)**

73 Zacchaeus

(Luke 19)

Thinking about God's Word

1. Why didn't Zacchaeus go home when he couldn't see Jesus because of the crowd? **(He wanted to see Jesus.)**

2. How do we know that Jesus was looking for Zacchaeus when He came to the tree? **(He looked up to where Zacchaeus was.)**

3. Why did some people mutter? **(Jesus went as the guest of a "sinner.")**

4. Was Jesus the guest of a sinner? Explain your answer. **(Zacchaeus, though a sinner, was completely forgiven by Jesus.)** Why did He go with Zacchaeus? **(to bring salvation to Zacchaeus and his house)**

5. Show how Zacchaeus's life was changed after he was found by Jesus and received Him as his Savior. **(Zacchaeus promised to give half of his possessions to the poor, and if he had cheated anybody out of anything, to pay back four times the amount.)**

Working with God's Word

Fill in the blanks.

1. Jesus passed through **Jericho**.

2. A man named Zacchaeus was a chief **tax collector**.

3. Zacchaeus showed that he was sorry for his sins by returning **four** times as much as he had gotten dishonestly.

4. Jesus said, "Today **salvation** has come to this house."

5. Jesus came to save what was **lost**.

Draw a line under the word that makes each sentence true.

1. Zacchaeus was very (old—kind—poor—**short**).

2. The people (shouted—**muttered**—rejoiced) when Jesus went into Zacchaeus's home.

3. Zacchaeus offered to give (all—**half**—most—one-third) of his possessions to the poor.

4. If he had stolen two dollars from a man, he would return (6—2—4—10—**8**—20) dollars to him.

5. Zacchaeus climbed a (maple—**sycamore**—pineapple) tree to see Jesus.

Applying God's Word

1. How did those who muttered show that they did not understand why Jesus had come to them? **(Jesus came for repentant sinners—those who recognize their sinfulness. Those who suppose themselves righteous apart from Him do not belong to Him since they do not recognize their need for the Savior.)**

2. In which words did Jesus give the reason for His coming into the world? **("For the Son of Man came to seek and to save what was lost.")**

3. What evidence does this account provide that the Holy Spirit changed the priorities in Zacchaeus's life after Jesus found him? **(Zacchaeus promised to give half of his possessions to the poor and four times the amount to anyone he had cheated.)**

74 The Lost Sheep and the Lost Coin
(Luke 15)

Thinking about God's Word

1. Who was gathering around to hear Jesus? **(tax collectors and sinners)**

2. Why do you think Jesus told parables? **(to help people understand and remember His teachings)**

3. Who is meant by the lost sheep of which Jesus spoke? **(sinners)**

4. When does a sinner cause joy in heaven? **(when the sinner repents)**

5. What is "the lost" in this parable? **(one sinner)**

Working with God's Word

Answer each question correctly with words from the story.

1. Whom did the teachers and Pharisees mutter about? **Jesus**

2. How many sheep were in the flock? **100**

3. How many sheep were lost? **1**

4. Who went to look for the sheep? **the shepherd**

5. Who is like the lost sheep? **a sinner**

Draw a line through each sentence that is not true. Write it correctly on the blank line that follows it.

1. ~~God wants only believers to be saved.~~
   (God wants all people to be saved.)

2. Jesus told the parable of the lost sheep.

3. Jesus welcomed sinners and ate with them.

4. ~~A good shepherd would rather lose one sheep than leave 99.~~
   (A good shepherd would rather leave 99 than lose one sheep.)

5. There is joy in heaven when a sinner repents.

6. The teachers and Pharisees did not know they were lost sheep.

7. The Son of Man is come to save that which was lost.

Applying God's Word

1. Who are the "righteous persons who do not need to repent"? **(self-righteous persons who do not think themselves in need of salvation)**

2. Were you ever a lost sheep? **(Yes)** When? **(before I was baptized and trusted in Jesus)** How did Jesus become your Shepherd? **(He found me and brought me to faith in Him.)**

3. How does God's Spirit move the followers of Jesus to show their care and concern for the lost? **(God's Spirit moves Jesus' followers to reach out to others with the Good News of the forgiveness, new life, and salvation Jesus won for us.)**

75 The Lost Son
(Luke 15)

Thinking about God's Word

1. What was the "share of the estate" the younger son got from his father? **(a portion of the father's property)**

2. What did the younger son do with his inheritance after he received it? **(He squandered it in wild living.)**

3. Find the words the son planned to use to say that he had sinned greatly and no longer deserved his father's love. Which words show that he had become humble? **("Father, I have sinned against heaven and against you. I am no longer worthy to be called your son; make me like one of your hired men.")**

4. How can you tell that he was truly sorry for what he had done? **(The story says that he came to his senses.)**

5. How did he confess his sin? **(He said, "Father, I have sinned against heaven and against you.")** How did he admit that he did not deserve forgiveness? **(He said, "I am no longer worthy to be called your son.")**

6. How did the father show that he had never stopped loving his son and that he had already forgiven him? **(He welcomed him back and celebrated his return.)** What did the father show by taking back his son as a member of his family? **(The father showed that he had forgiven him.)**

7. What did the father mean when he said, "For this son of mine was dead and is alive again"? **(The son was dead in sin, but was made alive through forgiveness and restored to the family.)**

Working with God's Word

Answer each question.
1. Who told this parable? **Jesus**
2. How did the son spend his goods? **He squandered his wealth in wild living.**
3. Why did the son feed pigs? **He had no other way to live.**

4. What kind of food would the son gladly have eaten? **the pods that the pigs were eating**

5. How can you tell that the father had been waiting for his son? **The father saw the son when he was still a long way off and ran out to meet him.**

6. Of whom is the father of this lesson a true picture? **God**

7. Of whom does the prodigal son remind you? **me**

Draw a circle around Yes or No.
1. Did the younger son ask for his portion of the possessions? **Yes** No

2. Did the prodigal son waste his money? **Yes** No

3. Did the son herd sheep during the famine? Yes **No**

4. Did the prodigal son know that he had sinned? **Yes** No

5. Does knowing that you have sinned bring forgiveness? Yes **No**

6. Did the father meet his son in a far country? Yes **No**

7. Was the prodigal son sorry for his sins? **Yes** No

Applying God's Word

1. When have you acted like the younger son? **(We act like the younger son when we turn our back on Jesus.)** the older son? **(We act like the older son when we think our worth or goodness makes us better than others.)**

2. Did the father like the son's bad deeds? **(No)** How did he show that he loved him just the same? **(He forgave the son and welcomed him back.)** How did the father's never-ending love help the son? **(He restored the son to the family and allowed him a new beginning.)**

3. Does God love the sins we do? **(No)** What can this parable mean to our lives? **(God always loves, forgives, and restores repentant sinners.)**

76 The Foolish Rich Man
(Luke 12)

Thinking about God's Word

1. What is an abundance of possessions? **(having many things, great wealth)**

2. What did the rich man want to do? **(tear down his barns and build bigger ones)**

3. What does "eat, drink and be merry" mean? **(take it easy and enjoy the good things in life)**

4. What was going to happen to the rich man? **(He would die.)**

5. What does Jesus say will happen to people who seek His kingdom? **(Material blessings will be there as well.)**

Working with God's Word

Answer each question.

1. What did Jesus tell His disciples to be on guard against? **all kinds of greed**

2. What produced a good crop for the rich man? **the ground**

3. What did the rich man want to do with his grain and goods? **Store them in the bigger barns he would build.**

4. What did God say would happen to the rich man that night? **He would die.**

5. What did Jesus tell His disciples not to worry about? **life, what they would eat or wear**

Cross out the false words. Rewrite the sentences to make them true.

1. "The Foolish Rich Man" is a ~~proverb~~.
   ("The Foolish Rich Man" is a parable.)

2. Jesus told this parable to the ~~children~~.
   (Jesus told this parable to the disciples)

3. God told the rich man that he would die that ~~weekend~~.
   (God told the rich man that he would die that night.)

4. Jesus told His disciples they ~~should~~ worry about their lives.
   (Jesus told His disciples they shouldn't worry about their lives.)

5. Jesus said that people should seek His kingdom ~~when they want~~.
   (Jesus said that people should seek His kingdom and all these things would be given to them as well.)

Applying God's Word

1. What was wrong with the priorities of the rich man? **(The rich man thought only of himself.)**

2. What does it mean to be "rich toward God"? **(To be rich toward God means to allow His Spirit to work in us so that we might live as His people, loving and serving both God and others.)**

3. Why do God's people not need to worry? **(God promises always to love, care for, and provide for us. He has already met our greatest needs through Christ Jesus.)**

77 The Pharisee and the Tax Collector

(Luke 18)

Thinking about God's Word

1. How did the Pharisee show that he thought himself righteous when he spoke his prayer? **(He thanked God he was righteous and then told of his righteous acts.)**

2. How did the Pharisee show in the words of his prayer that he despised others? **(He thanked God he was not like the tax collectors.)**

3. In which words did the Pharisee try to tell God of his good deeds instead of his sins? **("I fast twice a week and give a tenth of all I get.")** Why did he not ask for forgiveness of sins? **(He did not think he needed to be forgiven.)**

4. In whose wisdom, goodness, and righteousness did the tax collector put his trust? **(God's)**

5. What did the tax collector confess himself to be before God? **(a sinner)**

6. How did his actions show that he did not consider himself worthy to come to God? **(He bowed his head and beat his breast.)**

7. What was the only thing he asked of God? **("God, have mercy on me, a sinner.")**

8. Who trusted in himself to gain heaven? **the Pharisee**

9. Who trusted in God's mercy for salvation? **the tax collector**

Draw a line under the word or phrase that makes each sentence true.

1. The Bible tells of (two ways—many ways—**one way**) that it is possible for us to be saved.

2. We (can—**cannot**—sometimes can) be saved by our own deeds.

3. (One—**Two**—Three—Four) men went up to the temple to pray.

4. The (**tax collector**—Pharisee) thanked God that he was not like others.

5. The Pharisee fasted (once—**twice**—three times) a week.

6. The tax collector said he was a (Pharisee—child of God—**sinner**—son of Abraham).

7. The tax collector went down to his house (**justified**—condemned—lost).

Working with God's Word

Answer each question.

1. Which is the only way to heaven? **forgiveness through Jesus' righteousness**

2. How do some people wish to enter heaven? **by their own goodness or merit**

3. To whom did Jesus speak this parable? **to those confident of their own righteousness who look down on others**

4. Where did two men go to pray? **temple**

5. Who were the two men? **a Pharisee and a tax collector**

6. For what did the Pharisee thank God? **his goodness**

Applying God's Word

1. To whom did Jesus speak this parable? **(to those confident of their own righteousness who look down on everybody else)** What did they think of themselves? **(They were righteous.)** What did they think of others? **(They looked down on them.)**

2. Read the Pharisee's "prayer" carefully. For what did he ask God? **(nothing)**

3. What does it mean to be humble before God? **(to recognize and confess your sins)** How does God exalt the humble? **(God in Christ forgives our sins and makes us His own dear children through Christ Jesus, our Lord.)**

78 The Good Samaritan
(Luke 10)

Thinking about God's Word

1. What two questions did the expert in the law wish to have answered? (**"What must I do to inherit eternal life? Who is my neighbor?"**)

2. What happened to the man who was going from Jerusalem to Jericho? (**He fell into the hands of robbers.**) Which words tell that the wounded man had only a small chance to live? (**"leaving him half dead"**)

3. Who came down that road? (**a priest**)

4. Which words say that the Levite also passed the dying man without helping him? (**"passed by on the other side"**)

5. What did Jesus ask the expert in the law at the end of His parable? (**"Which of these three do you think was a neighbor to the man who fell into the hands of robbers?"**)

6. How did the expert in the law himself now answer the question he had asked Jesus? (**"the one who had mercy"**)

7. How did Jesus tell him to be a neighbor? (**"Go and do likewise."**)

Working with God's Word

Fill in the blanks.

1. Jesus told this parable to an **expert in the law**.

2. A man went down from Jerusalem to **Jericho**.

3. Robbers **took** his clothes.

4. A priest passed by on the **other** side when he saw him.

5. A **Levite** also looked on him and passed by.

6. A Samaritan had **pity** on him.

7. He poured oil and **wine** into his wounds.

8. He brought the wounded man to an **inn**.

9. The Samaritan said to the host, "**Look** after him."

10. Jesus said to the expert in the law, "Go and do **likewise**."

If a sentence is true, mark it T; if false, mark it F.

1. **F** While going to Jerusalem, a man fell into the hands of robbers.

2. **T** The man was stripped of his clothes and was left half dead.

3. **F** The priest and the Levite were true friends in need.

4. **F** The wounded man was the Good Samaritan.

5. **T** Jesus told this parable to teach the meaning of being a neighbor.

6. **T** A person who loves God truly will love his or her neighbor too.

Applying God's Word

1. In what ways was the Samaritan a neighbor to the wounded man? (**He came to where the man was, bandaged his wounds, took him to an inn, took care of him, and paid for his extended care.**)

2. What did the expert in the law not understand about himself relative to the Law? (**The expert did not recognize his inability to keep the Law.**)

3. How did Jesus prove Himself to be a good neighbor to us? (**Jesus did what we were unable to do for ourselves. He kept the Law perfectly in our place and died to pay the penalty we deserved for disobeying the Law.**)

79 The Triumphal Entry
(Matthew 21)

Thinking about God's Word

1. Why did Jesus send two disciples ahead to Bethphage? **(to get a donkey and her colt)** How was He going to use the animals? **(He was going to ride the donkey into Jerusalem.)**

2. Horses were used by soldiers and kings for warlike purposes. Donkeys were used in the everyday life of the people for moving people and things from place to place. How did Jesus show that He was coming to Jerusalem for a peaceful purpose? **(He rode a donkey rather than a horse.)**

3. Which prophecy was fulfilled when Jesus entered Jerusalem? **("Say to the Daughter of Zion, 'See, your king comes to you, gentle and riding on a donkey, on a colt, the foal of a donkey.' ")** What here is meant by the "Daughter of Zion"? **(the city of Jerusalem, which stands for the Christian church)** Who was the King who came to her? **(Jesus)**

4. What did the crowd do to honor Jesus as their King? **(They spread their cloaks and tree branches on the road and praised Him.)**

5. What did the people shout? **("Hosanna to the Son of David! Blessed is He who comes in the name of the Lord! Hosanna in the highest!")**

Working with God's Word

Fill the blanks with the correct words.

1. The disciples went to a city on the Mount of **Olives**.

2. Only **two** of Jesus' disciples were sent to find the donkey.

3. The disciples found the donkey in the city of **Bethphage**.

4. The disciples placed their **cloaks** on the donkey as a saddle.

5. The people cried, "**Hosanna** to the Son of David!"

6. Some honored Jesus by **spreading** tree branches on the road.

7. Others spread their **cloaks** on the road.

Draw a line under the correct answer to each question.

1. Toward which city were Jesus and His disciples going? (Capernaum—Bethlehem—**Jerusalem**—Jericho)

2. Which sad part of Jesus' life was soon to begin? (flight—preaching—**suffering**—ascension)

3. Which animal was found tied with the donkey? (**colt**—horse—sheep—watch dog)

4. Who spoke the words, "Say to the Daughter of Zion"? (the Lord—Moses—**a prophet**—the disciples)

5. Who rode on the donkey? (**Jesus**—the Daughter of Zion—the disciples)

6. What name did the multitude give to Jesus? (Hosanna—**Son of David**—Rabbi—Savior)

7. What did Jesus show Himself to be in this lesson? (**King**—Savior—mighty—rich—kind)

Applying God's Word

1. Explain the meaning of the designation "Son of David." **("Son of David" refers to the promised Messiah, the Son of David, who would come to bring victory to the people of God.)**

2. How did Jesus' words to His disciples show Him to be true God? **(Jesus told the disciples what they would find in the village.)**

3. Explain Jesus' purpose in going to Jerusalem. **(Jesus came to Jerusalem to suffer and die for the sins of all people.)**

80 The Anointing
(Mark 14; John 12)

Thinking about God's Word

1. In what city did the anointing take place? **(Bethany)**

2. Who served at the dinner for Jesus? **(Martha)**

3. Who was reclining at the table with Jesus? **(Lazarus)**

4. What did Mary do with the perfume? **(poured it on Jesus' feet)**

5. Why did the people there rebuke Mary? **(They thought it a waste of the expensive perfume.)**

6. Why did Jesus tell them to leave her alone? **(She was honoring Jesus when she had the opportunity.)**

7. What did Jesus say would be done in memory of Mary? **("Wherever the gospel is preached throughout the world, what she has done will also be told, in memory of her.")**

Working with God's Word

Fill in the blanks with a word from below.

1. Jesus arrived in Bethany **six** days before Passover.

2. A **dinner** was given in Jesus' honor.

3. Mary poured **perfume** on Jesus' feet.

4. She wiped His feet with her **hair**.

5. Some said, "Why this **waste** of perfume?"

6. Jesus said, "The poor you will **always** have with you."

7. The perfume was to prepare for Jesus' **burial**.

8. **Judas** betrayed Jesus.

dinner	use	always	hair
Judas	six	five	perfume
waste	burial		

Applying God's Word

1. How did Martha and Mary differ in the way they honored Jesus at the dinner? **(Martha served the dinner; Mary poured expensive perfume on Jesus' feet and wiped His feet with her hair as an act of worship.)**

2. Some well-intentioned believers may have been among those who criticized Mary's action. Explain. **(Tension always seems to exist between using resources to bring glory to God or to serve others.)**

3. Compare Mary's actions toward Jesus with those of Judas. **(Mary worshiped Jesus at great expense. Judas loved money; he sought to betray Jesus for financial gain.)**

Recalling God's Word

Match the following by drawing lines.

1. Jesus went to **(e)**
2. A dinner was given **(a)**
3. Martha **(g)**
4. Mary **(b)**
5. The perfume was **(d)**
6. Jesus' feet were wiped with **(c)**
7. Judas **(f)**

a. in Jesus' honor.
b. anointed Jesus' feet.
c. hair.
d. expensive.
e. Bethany.
f. went to betray Jesus.
g. served at the table.

81 The Last Judgment
(Matthew 25)

Thinking about God's Word

1. Will this world ever come to an end? **(Yes, when Jesus comes in His glory.)** According to this parable, who will sit on the throne of the kingdom of glory when the world comes to an end? **(the Son of Man—Jesus)**

2. Who will be gathered before Him? **(all nations)**

3. In which words will the righteous say that their righteousness is undeserved and not their own? **("Lord, when did we see You hungry and feed You, or thirsty and give You something to drink? When did we see You a stranger and invite You in, or needing clothes and clothe You? When did we see You sick or in prison and go to visit You?")**

4. Find the words in which the King, Jesus, says that when Christians, in faith, do good works, He counts the deeds as though they had been done to Him. **("I tell you the truth, whatever you did for one of the least of these brothers of Mine, you did for Me.")**

5. Whom will the King condemn into eternal fire? **(those on the left)** In Jesus' own words, why do they deserve this punishment? **("I was hungry and you gave Me nothing to eat, I was thirsty and you gave Me nothing to drink, I was a stranger and you did not invite Me in, I needed clothes and you did not clothe Me, I was sick and in prison and you did not look after Me.")**

6. In which words will the cursed say that the punishment is unfair? **("Lord, when did we see You hungry or thirsty or a stranger or needing clothes or sick or in prison, and did not help You?")**

7. How does the King tell those who are condemned that their own disobedience earned this punishment? **("I tell you the truth, whatever you did not do for one of the least of these, you did not do for Me.")**

8. Where will the wicked then go? **(into eternal fire prepared for the devil and his angels)**

9. Where will the righteous be taken? **(to their inheritance, the kingdom prepared for them)**

Working with God's Word

Answer each question on the blank line.

1. Who shall come with the Son of Man on Judgment Day? **all the angels**

2. To whom shall the King first speak? **those on His right**

3. Of which kindnesses will the King speak to all before Him? **feeding, giving water, showing hospitality, providing clothes, and visiting**

4. To whom will the King say, "Depart from Me, you who are cursed"? **those on the left**

5. Why will some be condemned to eternal fire? **They obviously have no faith.**

Fill in the blanks of the following sentence with words from below.

1. When the Son of Man comes on Judgment Day, all the holy **angels** shall come with Him.

2. All the **nations** will be gathered before Him.

3. First, the King shall speak to those at His **right** hand.

4. Whatever they have done to the least of His **brothers**, they have done to Him.

5. Afterward, the King shall speak to those on His **left** hand.

6. They must depart into eternal **fire**.

7. The **devil** and his angels will be with the wicked.

8. Those on the left will go into **eternal** punishment.

9. But the righteous will go into **life** eternal.

right	brothers	nations
left	eternal	life
devil	angels	priests
fire		

Applying God's Word

1. To whom will Jesus give the Kingdom? **(those who are blessed by His Father)** Why do they deserve to inherit the Kingdom? **(Jesus was hungry, thirsty, a stranger, in need of clothing, sick, and in prison, and they helped Him.)**

2. Who are Jesus' brothers? **(those who believe in Him as their Savior)**

3. How do we know from this parable that Jesus' followers do not do good works for the purpose of earning heaven? **(The righteous seem surprised that the good things they had done for others are mentioned.)**

82 The Lord's Supper
(Luke 22)

Thinking about God's Word

1. Which great Jewish festival was drawing near at this time? **(Passover)**

2. What were some of the preparations necessary according to Exodus 12:3–6? **("Tell the whole community of Israel that on the tenth day of this month each man is to take a lamb for his family, one for each household. If any household is too small for a whole lamb, they must share one with their nearest neighbor, having taken into account the number of people there are. You are to determine the amount of lamb needed in accordance with what each person will eat. The animals you choose must be year-old males without defect, and you may take them from the sheep or the goats. Take care of them until the fourteenth day of the month, when all the people of the community of Israel must slaughter them at twilight.")**

3. Whom did Jesus send to prepare the Passover? **(Peter and John)**

4. How did Jesus tell His disciples that this would be the last Passover? **("I have eagerly desired to eat this Passover with you before I suffer.")**

5. Which words show that Judas had become unfaithful before he went to the chief priests? **("Then Satan entered Judas.")**

6. As they were eating, what did Jesus give to His disciples? **(the Lord's Supper)** What did He tell them to do with it? **(to celebrate it in remembrance of Him)** What did He say it was? **(His body and blood)** For whom did Jesus say it was given? **("for you")** In whose memory were they to take it and eat it? **(in Jesus' memory)**

7. What did Jesus tell the disciples to do with the wine that was in the cup? **(drink it)**

Working with God's Word

On the blank lines tell of whom the following things are true.

1. Who told the disciples that the Son of Man would be crucified? **Jesus**

2. Who entered Judas Iscariot? **Satan**

3. Who went to the chief priests to betray Jesus? **Judas**

4. Who went with Peter to prepare the Passover? **John**

5. Who sat down with Jesus for the Passover meal? **the disciples**

6. Who said, "Take and eat; this is My body"? **Jesus**

7. Who said, "What are you willing to give me if I hand Him over to you?" **Judas**

Draw a line under the words that make the following sentences true.

1. The chief priests promised to give Judas (10 shekels of silver—gold—**30 silver coins**—great riches).

2. At the meal there were (10—11—12—**13**—9—15) people in all.

3. Jesus said that He desired to eat this Passover with the disciples before He (ascended—did more miracles—**suffered**—went to Galilee).

4. In the Lord's Supper Jesus gives us (bread and wine only—His true body and blood only—**His body and blood with the bread and wine**).

5. We partake of the Lord's Supper to remind us of (Jesus' birth—the children of Israel in the wilderness—Jesus' first miracle at Cana—**Jesus' suffering and death**).

Applying God's Word

1. Jesus broke the bread and gave it to His disciples. When was Jesus' body broken for us? **(Jesus' body was broken at Calvary, pierced by a spear upon His death.)**

2. Why was Passover a fitting time for Jesus to die for the sins of the world? **(At Passover a lamb was slaughtered in remembrance of God's deliverance of His people from bondage in Egypt. The slaughtering of the Passover lamb prefigured the sacrifice of Jesus for all sins.)**

3. For what purpose did Jesus pour out His blood? **(to earn our salvation)** Why should God's people receive the Lord's Supper often? **(We should receive the Sacrament often in obedience to Christ, to receive the assurance of forgiveness and the strengthening of faith it provides.)**

83 Jesus in Gethsemane
(Matthew 26; Luke 22)

Thinking about God's Word

1. Who led the way to the Mount of Olives? **(Jesus)**

2. How did Jesus warn His disciples about what they would all do that night? **(He said, "This very night you will all fall away on account of Me.")**

3. Which words describe the change that the disciples saw coming over Jesus? **("He began to be deeply distressed and troubled.")** Which words of Jesus describe His great sorrow? **("My soul is overwhelmed with sorrow to the point of death.")**

4. Whom did Jesus take with Him to Gethsemane? **(Peter, James, and John)**

5. What was the "cup" of which Jesus spoke to His Father? **(His suffering and death)**

6. How often did Jesus go to pray alone? **(three times)** With which words did He declare that He wanted God's will to be done? **("May Your will be done.")**

7. How many times did Jesus come to the three disciples who were to watch with Him? **(three times)** What did He find them doing each time? **(sleeping)** With which words did He admonish them the first time? **("Could you not keep watch for one hour? Watch and pray so that you will not fall into temptation. The spirit is willing, but the body is weak.")**

Working with God's Word

Answer each question correctly with one word or a short phrase.

1. Who said that he would never fall away from Jesus? **Peter**

2. How often would Peter disown Jesus that night? **three times**

3. What did Jesus ask the heavenly Father to take from Him? **"this cup"**

4. Which part of each disciple was very willing to help Jesus? **the spirit**

5. Which part of each disciple was weak? **the body**

6. Who came from heaven to strengthen Jesus? **an angel**

7. As what were the great drops of sweat that fell to the ground? **drops of blood**

If a sentence is true, write T; if it is false, write F.

1. **T** Jesus said that all the disciples would fall away that night.

2. **T** Peter trusted in himself not to disown Jesus.

3. **T** Jesus said that Peter would disown Him before the rooster would crow.

4. **T** Three disciples went into Gethsemane with Jesus.

5. **F** Simon Peter watched with Jesus in Gethsemane.

6. **T** Jesus prayed three times in the garden.

7. **T** While Jesus suffered greatly, the three disciples slept.

Applying God's Word

1. Where did Jesus go for strength as He anticipated His coming suffering? **(Jesus went to His heavenly Father in prayer as He sought strength for the ordeal ahead.)**

2. What did Jesus ask His disciples to pray about? **(Jesus asked His disciples to watch and pray so that they would not fall into temptation.)**

3. How did Jesus indicate His unwavering faithfulness to serve and obey His heavenly Father? **(Jesus prayed, "May Your will be done.")**

84 Jesus Is Betrayed and Arrested

(Matthew 26; John 18)

Thinking about God's Word

1. Who came with Judas to help in capturing Jesus? **(a large crowd sent from the chief priests and elders of the people)**

2. By which words did Jesus freely give Himself up to the mob? **("I am He.")**

3. How did Judas prove himself a hypocrite when he greeted and kissed Jesus? **(He greeted Jesus with "Greetings, Rabbi!")**

4. How did Jesus point out to Peter that there was a way of getting help from His Father if it were needed or wished for? **("Do you think I cannot call on My Father, and He will at once put at My disposal more than twelve legions of angels?")**

Working with God's Word

On the blank lines tell of whom the following things are true.

1. He said, "Who is it you want?" **Jesus**

2. They said, "Jesus of Nazareth." **the crowd**

3. His ear was cut off. **the high priest's servant**

4. He could send more than 72,000 angels to help Jesus. **God the Father**

5. They deserted Jesus and fled. **the disciples**

Applying God's Word

1. How did Peter try to save the situation? **(Peter drew his sword and struck the high priest's servant, cutting off his right ear.)** Why was this foolish as well as wrong? **(Jesus could have defended Himself if He so desired.)** By which words did Jesus teach that "the sword" (earthly force and power) has no place in God's plan for saving people from sin? **("All who draw the sword will die by the sword.")**

2. How did Jesus show Himself to be true God in this account? **(Jesus healed the ear of the high priest's servant.)**

3. Explain how Jesus showed His concern for His disciples even as He was being arrested? **(Jesus said, "If you are looking for Me, then let these men go.")**

Recalling God's Word

Match the following by drawing lines to join the parts that make a true sentence.

1. Judas came **(d)**

2. Jesus said to them, **(g)**

3. They drew back **(i)**

4. Judas said, **(e)**

5. The Savior said to Judas, **(k)**

6. The men seized Jesus **(a)**

7. The high priest's servant **(m)**

a. and arrested Him.

b. alone.

c. denied Jesus and fled.

d. with a crowd of people.

e. "Greetings, Rabbi!"

f. "Depart from Me!"

g. "Who is it you want?"

h. touched his ear and healed him.

i. and fell to the ground.

j. and worshiped Him.

k. "Are you betraying the Son of Man with a kiss?"

l. had a sword.

m. had his right ear cut off.

85 Jesus before the Sanhedrin
(Matthew 26; John 18)

Thinking about God's Word

1. Which words indicate that the chief priests, the elders, and the council didn't want to give Jesus a fair trial but had made up their minds to put Him to death even before they had questioned Him? (**"The chief priests and the whole Sanhedrin were looking for evidence against Jesus so that they could put Him to death."**) Why did Jesus' trial *have* to be an unfair one? **(He was without sin.)**

2. In which words did Caiaphas ask Jesus if He was the promised Messiah? (**"Tell us if You are the Christ, the Son of God."**) What did Jesus answer? (**"Yes, it is as you say."**)

3. What was the sin of blasphemy of which Jesus was said to be guilty? **(They said He claimed to be God.)** Was He guilty? **(No, Jesus is God.)**

Working with God's Word

Answer each question on the line.

1. Who was Caiaphas? **the high priest**

2. Who were assembled with Caiaphas? **the teachers of the law and the elders**

3. About which things did the high priest ask Jesus? **about His disciples and teaching**

4. Who struck Jesus? **one of the officials**

5. Why did the Sanhedrin seek evidence against Jesus? **They wanted to put Him to death.**

6. What did Caiaphas tell Jesus to tell him under oath by the living God? **"Tell us if You are the Christ, the Son of God."**

7. What did the high priest say of Jesus' answer? **"He has spoken blasphemy!"**

8. With which words did all the men of the Sanhedrin condemn Jesus? **"He is worthy of death."**

9. In which words did the soldiers mock Jesus after blindfolding Him? **"Prophesy to us, Christ. Who hit You?"**

Draw a line under the correct answer to each question.

1. To whom was Jesus led by the crowd? (Peter—Pontius Pilate—**Caiaphas**—Nicodemus)

2. Concerning what did the high priest ask Jesus? (hands and feet—**disciples and teaching**—mother and brethren)

3. To whom had Jesus spoken openly? (**the world**—believers only—all except Jews)

4. Who asked Jesus to take an oath? (a Roman officer—**the high priest**—Annas—Pontius Pilate)

5. Did Jesus ever take an oath? (no—**yes**—the Bible doesn't tell—every day)

6. Why was Jesus condemned to death by the Sanhedrin? (He had not obeyed Caesar—**He called Himself Christ**—He would not answer)

7. How did the men who held Jesus speak of Him? (very highly—they said only good things—**blasphemously**—kindly)

Applying God's Word

1. From what you yourself have learned of Jesus' life, cite with five or six phrases actions that indicate Jesus was the Christ, the Son of God. **(Jesus did miracles, fulfilled Old Testament prophecies, was identified as God's Son by His heavenly Father, was called God by His followers, and demonstrated the attributes of God. Answers will vary.)**

2. Why didn't Caiaphas believe Jesus when He said, "It is as you say"? **(He resisted the faith the Holy Spirit desired to work in his heart.)**

3. The Sanhedrin said of Jesus, "He is worthy of death." In what sense were their words inappropriate? **(Jesus was innocent of any wrongdoing.)** In what sense were these words true and appropriate? **(Jesus took our sins upon Himself in order to pay for them on our behalf. Therefore, He was guilty—in our place.)**

Peter Disowns Jesus; Judas Dies
(Matthew 26–27; Luke 22; John 18)

Thinking about God's Word

1. To deny means that a person does not want to admit or confess something. What did Peter first deny? **(being one of Jesus' disciples)** Why was that a sin? **(Denying belonging to Jesus is the same as denying Him as Lord and breaking the First Commandment.)**

2. To deny a person means to disown him or not want to know him. In which words did Peter deny Jesus? **("I don't know this man you're talking about.")** Why was that a sin? **(Honoring yourself before God breaks the First Commandment.)**

3. What was the third denial? **(Peter denied knowing Jesus.)** What sins did Peter add to that of denial? **(He cursed and swore, breaking also the Second Commandment.)**

4. How did Jesus call Peter to repentance? **(Jesus simply looked at Peter.)** Which words describe Peter's great sorrow over his sin? **("Peter remembered the word the Lord had spoken to him: 'Before the rooster crows today, you will disown Me three times.' And he went outside and wept bitterly.")**

5. Which words speak of the sorrow that Judas felt when he saw that Jesus was condemned? **("He was seized with remorse and returned the thirty silver coins to the chief priests and the elders. 'I have sinned,' he said, 'for I have betrayed innocent blood.' ")**

6. What did the priests say to Judas? **("What is that to us? That's your responsibility.")**

7. How did Judas let unbelief rob him of life? **(He committed suicide.)**

Working with God's Word

Fill in the blanks correctly.

1. Peter stood with the servants and officers to see the **outcome**.

2. The **girl** who kept the door said Peter was a disciple.

3. Peter **denied** that he was a disciple.

4. Peter denied **three** times.

5. Judas repented and brought the **30** silver coins to the priests.

6. Judas said he had betrayed **innocent** blood.

7. Finally, Judas went and **hanged** himself.

Draw a line under the correct answer to each question.

1. To which place had Peter followed Jesus? (Galilee—temple—Herod's palace—**high priest's palace**)

2. How many times did Peter deny that he knew Jesus? (1—2—**3**)

3. How could it be known that Peter was from Galilee? (by his clothing—**by his accent**—by his face—by his age)

4. How was Peter reminded of Jesus' warning? (by a word—**by a look**—by a girl—by a sword)

5. How did Peter show his repentance? (**he wept**—he went to the priests—he left Jesus—he went home)

6. How did Judas show sorrow for his sin? (he cried—he went to Jesus—**he gave back the silver**—he bought a field)

7. With what sin did all the sins of Judas end? (adultery—coveting—cursing—**suicide**—swearing)

Applying God's Word

1. Explain the difference between the sorrow of Peter and the sorrow of Judas. **(Both Peter and Judas were sorry for what they had done. Peter turned to Jesus for the forgiveness He offers freely. Peter's sorrow brought repentance. Judas turned away from Jesus, and in despair took his own life.)**

2. What evidence can you cite from this account that one sin leads to another? **(Moved by greed, Judas betrayed his Lord. When seized with the realization of what he had done, Judas committed suicide.)**

3. How do God's people today deny Jesus as their Savior? **(Answers will vary. Possibilities include people pretending they are not followers of Christ in order to fit in with a certain group or in other ways failing to live as a child of God.)**

87 Jesus before Pilate

(Matthew 27; John 18)

Thinking about God's Word

1. What charges did the Sanhedrin bring against Jesus? **(They charged Jesus with blasphemy and with subverting the nation.)** Why was this a serious charge before the Roman governor? **(Rome held the Jewish nation in submission. The charge might be perceived as a threat to Pilate.)**

2. By which words did Jesus make Pilate curious about His kingdom? **("My kingdom is not of this world.")** How did Jesus answer the question as to whether He is a king? **("You are right in saying I am a king. In fact, for this reason I was born, and for this I came into the world, to testify to the truth. Everyone on the side of truth listens to Me.")**

3. In which words did Jesus tell Pilate why He had come into the world? **("For this reason I was born, and for this I came into the world, to testify to the truth. Everyone on the side of truth listens to Me.")**

4. In which words did Pilate declare Jesus guiltless? **("I find no basis for a charge against Him.")** How did he in the same breath treat Jesus as one who deserved punishment? **(Pilate added, "Therefore, I will punish Him and then release Him.")** Was that just? **(No)** Why? **(An innocent man should not receive punishment.)**

5. How did the people show that they wanted Jesus to be put to death? **(They shouted, "Crucify Him! Crucify Him!")**

6. What unfair treatment did Pilate let the soldiers give Jesus even when he knew that Jesus was without fault? **(Pilate allowed Jesus to be flogged, tortured, mocked, and humiliated.)**

7. How did the chief priests and officers show only blind hatred in their hearts for Jesus? **(They insisted Jesus be crucified.)**

Working with God's Word

Answer each question with Yes or No.

1. Did the Sanhedrin deliver Jesus to Caiaphas, the governor? **No**

2. Did the Sanhedrin call Jesus guilty because He had been subverting the nation? **Yes**

3. Did Pilate ask Jesus, "Are You the king of the Jews?" **Yes**

4. Did Pilate say, "I have found many faults in this man"? **No**

5. Did Pilate want to release Jesus? **Yes**

6. Did the priests, rulers, and people want to release Jesus? **No**

7. Did Pilate have Jesus flogged? **Yes**

8. Did the people want Pilate to crucify Jesus? **Yes**

Draw a line under the words that make each sentence true.

1. Pilate was the (high priest—**governor**—king).

2. The people accused Jesus of calling Himself (Caesar—God—**a king**—Governor).

3. Pilate asked Jesus if He were a (God—**king**—Christian—Roman).

4. Jesus (**was**—wasn't) a king.

5. Pilate soon found out that Jesus (was guilty—was true God—**was innocent**—was the Savior of the world).

6. The crown that Jesus wore was made of (**thorns**—gold—purple—reeds).

7. When Pilate brought Jesus forth, he said, ("Crucify Him!"—"Flog Him!"—**"Here is the man!"**—"Scourge Him!").

8. Pilate washed his hands to show that (Jesus was innocent—**he was innocent**—the Jews were innocent).

9. At last Pilate said that Jesus should be (put into prison—**crucified**—set free—sent to Rome).

Applying God's Word

1. How does Jesus' kingship differ from that which Pilate had in mind as he questioned Jesus? **(Jesus is the Lord and ruler of the universe. Pilate envisioned someone seeking to establish Himself as the leader of a Jewish insurrectionist movement.)**

2. Since Pilate declared Jesus to be innocent, why did he not set Him free? **(He wanted to appease the people.)** How did he try to "wash his hands" of Jesus' blood? **(Pilate actually washed his hands, declaring to Jesus' accusers that they must bear the responsibility for Jesus' death.)** Who asked that the punishment for this day's evil deeds come upon them? **(all the people)** Actually, who paid for the sins of Pilate and Jesus' accusers? **(Jesus Himself)**

3. Explain how and why Jesus suffered under Pontius Pilate. **(Jesus was mocked, humiliated, and tortured under Pilate. Pilate sought to punish Jesus so that the people would be moved to have compassion on Him and seek His release. Jesus suffered under Pilate for the sins we committed.)**

88 Jesus Is Crucified
(Luke 23; John 19)

Thinking about God's Word

1. How did the soldiers carry out the will of the Jewish leaders by order of the governor? **(They led Jesus away to be crucified.)**

2. How do we know that even in His great agony Jesus thought of the welfare of His mother? **(Jesus asked John to care for His mother.)** Who was to take care of her from now on? **(John)**

3. Which prayer to Jesus shows that one of the criminals repented in his dying hour? **("Jesus, remember me when You come into Your kingdom.")** What certain promise did Jesus give him? **("I tell you the truth, today you will be with Me in paradise.")**

Working with God's Word

Fill in the blanks.

1. Jesus carried His own **cross** when He went to be crucified.

2. He went to a place called **Golgotha**.

3. Two **others (criminals)** were crucified with Jesus.

4. One criminal said, "Aren't You the **Christ**? Save Yourself and us!"

5. Darkness came over the land at the **sixth** hour.

Circle Yes or No.

1. A soldier carried Jesus' body.   Yes   **No**

2. Jesus asked God to bring revenge upon His enemies.   Yes   **No**

3. Two criminals were crucified with Jesus. **Yes**   No

4. The darkness over the land began at the third hour.   Yes   **No**

5. Jesus asked Peter to care for His mother, Mary. Yes   **No**

Applying God's Word

1. With which prayer did Jesus ask forgiveness for those who had brought Him to His death? **("Father, forgive them, for they do not know what they are doing.")** In what way does this prayer also include you? **(Jesus died for all sins, including mine.)**

2. What did Jesus cry out at the ninth hour? **("My God, My God, why have You forsaken Me?")** Which words show that this may have been the time of His greatest suffering? **("Jesus cried out in a loud voice.")** Because of whose sins had God forsaken Him? **(All sins, including ours.)**

3. What knowledge did one of the criminals on the cross have of the Christ? **(One of the criminals knew that the Christ would be powerful. He taunted, "Aren't You the Christ? Save Yourself and us!")** What knowledge did he lack? **(The criminal failed to recognize Jesus as the Savior from sin, death, and the devil's power.)**

89 Jesus Dies and Is Buried

(Matthew 27; Luke 23; John 19)

Thinking about God's Word

1. What was Jesus given to drink? **(wine vinegar)**

2. What did Jesus say after He drank? **("It is finished.")**

3. What did Jesus say before He died? **("Father, into Your hands I commit My spirit.")**

4. How did one member of the council show honor to Jesus' body? **(He asked for Jesus' body.)** How did another man show his love for Jesus openly? **(Nicodemus helped Joseph prepare Jesus' body for burial.)**

5. How did the very fact that they were anointing Jesus show that these friends had not understood what Jesus had spoken of in Luke 18:31–34? **(Jesus said He would rise again from the dead. They anointed Jesus' body because they thought he was dead forever.)**

6. After burying His body, how did the friends of Jesus make His grave secure? **(They rolled a big stone in front of the entrance to the tomb.)** How did God use the enemies of Jesus to make the grave still more secure? **(At the urging of the chief priests and Pharisees, Pilate put a seal on the stone and posted a guard at the tomb.)**

7. The chief priests and Pharisees did not believe Jesus would rise. Why then did they want His grave guarded? **(They feared the disciples would remove Jesus' body and then claim He had risen from the dead.)**

Working with God's Word

Answer the questions correctly on the blank lines.

1. Why did the Jewish leaders want the legs of those who had been crucified broken? **to hasten death**

2. Why were Jesus' legs not broken? **Jesus was already dead.**

3. How did the soldiers make sure that Jesus was dead? **One of the soldiers pierced Jesus' side with a spear.**

4. Which women saw where Jesus was laid? **Mary Magdalene and Mary the mother of Joses, Mark 15:47**

5. What did the women do on the Sabbath Day? **rested and worshiped God**

6. Who met with Pilate the next day? **the chief priests and Pharisees**

7. How did Jesus' enemies make the tomb secure? **They brought their concerns to Pilate, who sealed the tomb and posted a guard.**

Write T if the sentence is true; write F if the sentence is false.

1. **F** Nicodemus asked that the legs of the crucified men be broken.

2. **T** The soldiers broke the two criminals' legs.

3. **F** Jesus' legs were pierced with a spear.

4. **T** Joseph of Arimathea was a follower of Jesus.

5. **T** Nicodemus brought a mixture of myrrh and aloes.

6. **F** Jesus' 11 disciples buried Him.

7. **T** The friends of Jesus rested on the Sabbath Day.

8. **T** Jesus' enemies knew that He had said, "After three days I will rise again."

9. **F** Pilate gave the disciples a guard.

10. **F** Jesus' disciples sealed the stone.

Applying God's Word

1. Why were Jesus' legs not broken? See Numbers 9:12. **(None of the bones of the Passover lamb were to be broken.)**

2. How did the piercing of Jesus' side fulfill a prophecy of the Old Testament? See Zechariah 12:10. **(Zechariah 12:10 says, "They will look on Me, the one they have pierced.")**

3. What did Jesus accomplish for us through His death? **(Through His death Jesus won victory for us over sin, death, and Satan's power.)**

90 The Resurrection of Christ
(Matthew 28; Mark 16)

Thinking about God's Word

1. On what day had Jesus died? **(Friday)** During which full day was He dead? **(Saturday)** How can you tell that it was now the third day? **(The Sabbath was over. It was very early on the first day of the week.)**

2. Why did the women go to the tomb? **(to anoint Jesus' body)** What question did they ask on the way? **("Who will roll the stone away from the entrance to the tomb?")**

3. Who had already rolled the stone away? **(an angel)** Who became alarmed when they saw him? **(the women)**

4. To whom did Mary Magdalene run when she saw that the stone was rolled away? **(Peter and the other disciple—the one Jesus loved, John)** What did she think? **(someone had taken Jesus' body)**

5. With what glorious message did the angel explain the empty grave? **("He has risen!")**

6. To whom were the women to tell the glad news first? **(the disciples)** Whose name was especially mentioned? **(Peter)**

7. Where would the disciples see Jesus with their own eyes? **(in Galilee)**

Working with God's Word

Answer each question with one or two words.

1. Of whom is it said that they shook and became like dead men? **the guards**

2. Who said, "They have taken the Lord out of the tomb"? **Mary Magdalene**

3. Who was the disciple whom Jesus loved? **John**

4. Who said, "He has risen! He is not here"? **the angel**

5. Who entered the tomb and saw a young man? **the women**

Answer each question by circling Yes or No.

1. Did the women go to the grave on the Sabbath Day? Yes **No**

2. Is Sunday the first day of the week? **Yes** No

3. Did the angel roll the stone away to let Jesus out? Yes **No**

4. Did Salome tell Peter and John that the tomb was empty? Yes **No**

5. Did all the women enter Jesus' tomb? Yes **No**

6. Was an angel in the tomb? **Yes** No

7. Did Jesus arise from the dead on Sunday? **Yes** No

8. Did the disciples steal Jesus' body? Yes **No**

9. Was Jesus in the grave until the third day? **Yes** No

10. Did Jesus break the chains of death for us? **Yes** No

Applying God's Word

1. How do you know the women did not expect Jesus to rise from the dead? **(The women carried spices with them to the tomb so that they might anoint Jesus' body.)**

2. Why were the women afraid, yet joyful, as they left the empty tomb? **(No doubt they were afraid after seeing the angel, yet they were joyful at the message the angel brought them.)**

3. Read the entire message of the angel. Note how many things he said in those few words. What are they? ("You are looking for Jesus the Nazarene, who was crucified. He has risen! He is not here. See the place where they laid Him. But go, tell His disciples and Peter, 'He is going ahead of you into Galilee. There you will see Him, just as He told you.' ") Which is the most important to you? (Answers will vary.)

91 The First Appearances of the Risen Lord
(Matthew 28; John 20)

Thinking about God's Word

1. Who were the first people to whom the risen Lord appeared? **(the women)**

2. Why did Mary not recognize Jesus at first? **(She had been crying.)** What did she say when Jesus said her name? **("Rabboni!" which means Teacher.)**

3. What message did Jesus tell her to give the disciples? **("I am returning to My Father and your Father, to My God and your God.")**

4. What did Jesus call the disciples? **("My brothers")** What did this show about His love for them, even though they had forsaken Him three days ago? **(He still loved them and forgave them for abandoning Him.)**

5. How did the words *go* and *tell* show that Jesus was thinking of others who were fearful and needed comfort? **(He wanted others to know the good news of His victory over sin, death, and Satan.)**

Working with God's Word

Each sentence below has one mistake in it. Draw a line through the wrong word and write the correct one in its place.

1. Mary stood near the tomb, sleeping. **(sleeping to crying)**

2. Peter asked her whom she was seeking. **(Peter to Jesus)**

3. Mary thought that Jesus was an angel. **(an angel to the gardener)**

4. Rabboni means "Messiah." **(Messiah to Teacher)**

5. Mary Magdalene told the women that she had seen the Lord. **(women to disciples)**

6. Jesus met the women and said to them, "All glory!" **("All glory!" to "Greetings.")**

7. They held Jesus by the feet, and they kissed Him. **(kissed to worshiped)**

8. The guards told the chief officers all the things that had happened. **(officers to priests)**

9. The soldiers were paid to say, "His enemies came during the night and stole Him away." **(enemies to disciples)**

Draw a line under the words that make each sentence true.

1. Jesus said to her, ("Greetings!"—"Rabboni"—**"Mary"**—"Don't cry").

2. Mary said to Jesus, ("Greetings"—**"Rabboni"**—"Mary"—"Don't cry").

3. Mary Magdalene told (Jesus' mother—**the disciples**—the women—the chief priests) that she had seen Jesus.

4. The (disciples—**guards**—women—Pharisees) told the chief priests what had been done at the grave.

5. The soldiers were given (promises—punishment—**money**) to lie.

Applying God's Word

1. Why was Mary not with the other women to hear the angel's message? **(Mary had gone back to tell the disciples that Jesus' body was missing from the tomb.)**

2. How did the women respond when they met the resurrected Christ? **(They clasped His feet and worshiped Him.)**

3. Mary didn't recognize the risen Jesus until Jesus spoke to her. How does Jesus speak to people today to bring them to recognize Himself as their Lord and Savior? **(Jesus works through Word and Sacraments to impart and strengthen faith in Him.)**

92 Christ Appears to His Disciples
(John 20; Matthew 28)

Thinking about God's Word

1. When did Jesus appear to His disciples? **(Sunday evening)** What was the disciples' reaction? **(They were startled and frightened, thinking they saw a ghost.)**

2. With which words did Jesus greet the disciples? **("Peace be with you.")**

3. How did Jesus now let the doubting disciples convince themselves that He was really the same Jesus who had lived among them before His death? **(He invited them to examine His wounds.)** Read the words that show that the disciples now believed. **("The disciples were overjoyed when they saw the Lord.")**

4. As the risen Lord who would live forever, Jesus gave His servants a last command. What are the words of this important commission? **("All authority in heaven and on earth has been given to Me. Therefore go and make disciples of all nations, baptizing them in the name of the Father and of the Son and of the Holy Spirit, and teaching them to obey everything I have commanded you. And surely I am with you always, to the very end of the age.")**

5. From the Great Commission, write the words that tell

   a. that the One giving the command is the Lord of heaven and earth; **("All authority in heaven and on earth has been given to Me.")**

   b. that the disciples were to go to others instead of waiting for them to come to them; **("Therefore go")**

   c. who was to go; **("You")**

   d. what they were to do; **("Make disciples of all nations, baptizing them in the name of the Father and of the Son and of the Holy Spirit, and teaching them to obey everything I have commanded.")**

   e. whom they were to teach and baptize; **("all nations")**

   f. in whose name they were to baptize; **("in the name of the Father and of the Son and of the Holy Spirit")**

   g. what things they should teach. **("everything I have commanded you")**

Working with God's Word

Fill in the blanks.

1. The doors were **locked** for fear of the Jews.

2. Jesus said unto them, "Why are you **troubled**?"

3. He **showed** them His hands and His feet.

4. The **disciples** were overjoyed when they saw the Lord.

5. Jesus **breathed** on His disciples.

6. Then the 11 **disciples** went into Galilee.

7. There they worshiped Him, but some **doubted**.

8. Jesus said, "Go and make disciples of all **nations**."

9. Jesus said, "I am with you **always**."

Fill in the blanks with words from below.

1. Jesus came to His disciples on the **first** day of the week.

2. Jesus stood among them and said, "**Peace** be with you."

3. The disciples thought that they saw a **ghost**.

4. Jesus said, "A ghost does not have **flesh and bones**."

5. Jesus said, "If you forgive anyone his **sins**, they are forgiven."

first	body and blood	flesh and bones
peace	ghost	second
sins	nations	

Applying God's Word

1. By what sign did Jesus show that He was now giving them the Holy Spirit? **(He breathed on them.)** What important power did He give them? **(power to forgive sins and to withhold forgiveness)**

2. With which words did Jesus now remind them that He was no longer the humble Servant, but the exalted Lord of heaven and earth? **("All authority in heaven and on earth has been given to Me.")**

3. What tasks did Jesus give His disciples after His resurrection? **(Jesus told His disciples to forgive and retain sins and to go and make disciples of all nations, baptizing them in the name of the Father and of the Son and of the Holy Spirit, teaching them to obey everything He commanded.)**

93 The Ascension

(Acts 1)

Thinking about God's Word

1. In which words did Jesus promise a special gift to His disciples? **("Wait for the gift My Father promised.")** Where were they to wait until He sent it? **(Jerusalem)** Which words tell what the gift would be? **("You will be baptized with the Holy Spirit.")**

2. Where did Jesus lead His disciples after He had spoken to them? **(the vicinity of Bethany)** Why did He lift up His hands? **(to bless them)**

3. How did God's messengers announce that Jesus will come again? **("This same Jesus, who has been taken from you into heaven, will come back in the same way you have seen Him go into heaven.")**

4. How do you know the disciples understood the words of the angels? **(They worshiped Him and returned to Jerusalem with great joy.)**

Working with God's Word

Answer each question Yes or No.

1. Is Jesus' resurrection absolutely true? **Yes**

2. Did Jesus say, "Wait for the gift My Father promised"? **Yes**

3. Did John baptize with water? **Yes**

4. Did Jesus ask the disciples to stay in Bethany? **No**

5. Did Jesus and His disciples go to Bethany? **Yes**

6. Did Jesus bless His disciples before He left them? **Yes**

7. Were two men standing by the disciples as Jesus ascended? **Yes**

8. Will Jesus come again in the same way as He ascended? **Yes**

9. Did the disciples worship the angels before returning? **No**

Cross out the sentences that are not true. Write them correctly on the blanks.

1. Jesus lived on earth 40 years after His resurrection. **Jesus lived on earth 40 days after His resurrection.**

2. The disciples were to leave Jerusalem and start preaching immediately. **The disciples were to stay in Jerusalem and wait for the promised gift.**

3. Jesus ascended into heaven at Bethany.

4. Twelve disciples saw Jesus ascend. **Eleven disciples saw Jesus ascend.**

5. An angel stood by the disciples as Jesus ascended. **Two angels stood by the disciples as Jesus ascended.**

6. Jesus now sits at the right hand of God.

7. We will see Jesus someday.

8. The disciples were sad when they returned to Jerusalem. **The disciples were joyful when they returned to Jerusalem.**

Applying God's Word

1. Why did Jesus show Himself on earth after He had proven His power over death and the devil? **(to prove He was indeed alive)**

2. In what way was Jesus no longer to be with His disciples? **(physically)** In what way would He remain with them all the time? **(His Spirit would always remain with them.)**

3. How did the disciples respond after Jesus' ascension? **(They worshiped Him.)** How are Jesus' disciples still responding in the same way today? **(Believers still gather to worship and praise the risen Christ.)**

94 The Holy Spirit Comes at Pentecost
(Acts 2)

Thinking about God's Word

1. What signs indicated the Holy Spirit entered the room in which the disciples were gathered? **(a sound like the blowing of a violent wind and the appearance of tongues of fire on the heads of Jesus' followers)** What showed that the Spirit had entered the disciples? **(Tongues of fire came to rest on each of them.)**

2. By what miracle did the disciples show that the Holy Spirit had come upon them? **(They began to speak in other tongues as the Spirit enabled them.)** Which words tell that the Holy Spirit told them what to say? **("as the Spirit enabled them")**

3. Which words of the people give us an idea of what things the disciples preached? **("declaring the wonders of God")**

4. What did some in the crowd say of this Pentecost miracle? **("They have had too much wine.")** Why? **(They didn't believe God had blessed Jesus' followers with a special outpouring of the Spirit's power.)**

5. Tell how Peter began the work of "catching men" that Jesus had foretold in Matthew 4:18–19. **(He preached a powerful sermon.)**

6. Read Peter's words. According to Peter, what did Jesus' miracles, His suffering and death, and His resurrection prove Him to be? **("both Lord and Christ")** Why could Peter be so sure of Jesus' power to do miracles, of His death, and of His resurrection? **(Peter had witnessed all of these things himself.)**

7. How can you tell that Peter was now filled with the Holy Spirit? **(He was bold and direct in his proclamation of Christ, in contrast to the time in the courtyard when he denied Jesus.)**

Working with God's Word

On the blank lines tell of whom the following things are true.

1. He gave the disciples power to speak in other tongues. **Holy Spirit**

2. God-fearing people were there from every nation under heaven. **Jerusalem**

3. They were all amazed and bewildered. **Jews from every nation**

4. They said, "They have had too much wine." **some who made fun of the disciples**

5. He said, "Men of Israel, listen to this." **Peter**

6. He told the people to repent and to be baptized. **Peter**

7. People must repent and be baptized in His name. **Jesus Christ**

Draw a line under the words that make each sentence true.

1. The disciples began to speak in other (voices—fires—**tongues**).

2. (**The Holy Spirit**—The Son—The Father) came upon the disciples.

3. Jesus had been accredited by God by (the Jews—everyone—**miracles**).

4. (Peter—**The Holy Spirit**—The disciples) opened the hearts of the people so that they repented.

5. About (30,000—300,000—**3,000**—300) people became Christians that day.

Applying God's Word

1. For what purpose was the Spirit's power released at Pentecost? **(So that the Gospel might be preached with understanding and power and so that people might come to faith in Jesus.)**

2. Which words show that the people were sorry for what they had done? **("When the people heard this, they were cut to the heart and said to Peter and the other apostles, 'Brothers, what shall we do?' ")** How did Peter tell them they could obtain forgiveness for all their sins? **("Repent and be baptized, every one of you, in the name of Jesus Christ for the forgiveness of your sins. And you will receive the gift of the Holy Spirit. The promise is for you and your children and for all who are far off—for all whom the Lord our God will call.")** How did the Lord bless the words spoken by Peter? **("Those who accepted his message were baptized, and about three thousand were added to their number that day.")**

3. Who is included among the recipients of God's promise in Christ Jesus? **(Believers living today are included in the phrase "all who are far off.")**

95 The Crippled Beggar Is Healed

(Acts 3)

Thinking about God's Word

1. Why was the crippled man at the gate of the temple? **(He came there to beg every day.)** Why was the temple the best place to which people could be brought if they needed mercy from other people? **(Many came and went at the temple. Some honored God by giving gifts to the poor.)**

2. What did the lame man expect of Peter and John? **(money)**

3. What did the lame man receive that was better than silver and gold? **(healing)**

4. How did the man show his thankfulness for what he had received? **(He went into the temple courts with Peter and John, walking and jumping and praising God.)**

5. From which words can you see the reason for performing this miracle at the time and in the place it was done? **("When all the people saw him walking and praising God, they were filled with wonder and amazement at what had happened to him.")**

Working with God's Word

Answer each question with one word or a short phrase.

1. At what time was the crippled man healed? **at three in the afternoon**

2. Who took the crippled man by the hand and helped him up? **Peter**

3. Whom did the crippled man praise? **God**

4. Who saw the crippled man walking? **the people**

5. Who spoke to the people? **Peter**

Draw a line under the words that make each sentence true.

1. The disciple with Peter was named (Andrew—**John**—James—Philip).

2. The man could walk again (in the same hour—the next day—**immediately**—soon afterward).

3. The man was healed by (Peter's—John's—**God's**—Peter and John's) power.

4. The first place that the healed man went was (to his wife—to Jesus—home—**to the temple courts**).

5. The people who saw this miracle were brought to Christ by (the miracle—the crippled man—**God's Word**—the crowd).

6. After Peter's sermon the number of male believers grew to about (3,000—4,000—**5,000**—10,000).

Applying God's Word

1. To whom did Peter and John give all glory for the miracles? **(God)** In which words did Peter tell the people what they had done? **("You killed the Author of life.")** How did he offer the love and forgiveness of Jesus to all? **(He told the people to repent.)** Who were the ones who received forgiveness? **(those who believed)**

2. What words of God's Law did Peter preach? **(Peter told the people that they had caused the Son of God to suffer and die.)**

3. What were Peter's words of Gospel? **(Peter invited the people to "turn to God, so that your sins may be wiped out, that times of refreshing may come from the Lord.")** What results does God work in people through the Gospel? **(God gives forgiveness, faith for a new life, and eternal salvation through the Gospel.)**

96 Stephen

(Acts 6–8)

Thinking about God's Word

1. According to Acts 6:1–5, what was Stephen's work? **(Stephen was one of the seven responsible for caring for the widows.)**

2. Which words tell why Stephen could do miracles? **(He was "a man full of God's grace and power.")**

3. Who stirred up the people against Stephen? **(members of the Synagogue of the Freedmen)** What accusations did they bring against him? **("This fellow never stops speaking against this holy place and against the law.")**

4. Read Stephen's reply to the accusations against him. How had the fathers of the Jews been stiff-necked? **(They resisted the Holy Spirit.)** Who was the Righteous One who had been betrayed and murdered? **(Jesus)**

5. Which words of the lesson tell that Stephen's words upset his accusers? **("They were furious and gnashed their teeth at him.")**

6. Why could Stephen look into heaven? **(He was full of the Holy Spirit.)** Whom could he see there? **(Jesus, standing at the right hand of God)**

7. Whose name is mentioned as being pleased with Stephen's death? **(Saul)**

Working with God's Word

Fill in the blanks.

1. Stephen did great **wonders and miraculous signs** among the people.

2. People produced false **witnesses** against Stephen.

3. Stephen said the people were murderers of the **Righteous** One.

4. The men were **furious** and gnashed their teeth at him.

5. They rushed at him and **dragged** him out of the city.

6. Then they **stoned** Stephen.

7. **Saul** gave approval to his death.

Write a T or F in the blank.

1. **T** Stephen was a man full of God's grace and power.

2. **T** Stephen did great wonders among the people.

3. **F** Those who argued with Stephen found it simple to disprove what he taught.

4. **F** The men who testified against Stephen were honest men.

5. **F** When Stephen spoke to the Sanhedrin, his face shone like the sun.

6. **F** A young man named Saul tried to save Stephen from the hands of the mob.

7. **F** When Stephen died, he asked God to bring revenge upon his murderers.

Applying God's Word

1. What words of God's Law did Stephen speak? **(Stephen accused the people of being stiff-necked, of resisting the Holy Spirit, of persecuting the prophets, and of betraying and murdering the Messiah.)** With what result? **(The people stoned Stephen.)**

2. With which simple prayer did Stephen place his soul into the hands of his Lord? **("Lord Jesus, receive my spirit.")**

3. How did Stephen's last prayer show his enemies that he had a real interest in the salvation of their souls? **(He prayed, "Lord, do not hold this sin against them.")**

97 Philip and the Ethiopian
(Acts 8)

Thinking about God's Word

1. Where did the angel tell Philip to go? (**"South to the road—the desert road—that goes down from Jerusalem to Gaza"**)

2. Whom did Philip meet on the way? (**an Ethiopian eunuch, an important officer**)

3. What did the Spirit tell Philip to do? (**"Go to that chariot and stay near it."**)

4. What did Philip ask the man? (**"Do you understand what you are reading?"**)

5. What did Philip do with water? (**baptized the man**)

6. What happened to Philip? (**The Spirit of God suddenly took him away.**)

7. What did the man do? (**He went on his way rejoicing.**)

Working with God's Word

Fill in the blanks with words from the story.

1. Philip went south on the road that went from Jerusalem to **Gaza**.

2. The Ethiopian had gone to **Jerusalem** to worship.

3. The Ethiopian was reading the Book of **Isaiah**.

4. He asked **Philip** to come sit with him.

5. Philip told the Ethiopian the good news about **Jesus**.

6. The **Spirit** of the Lord took Philip away.

7. The Ethiopian went on his way **rejoicing**.

Put these events in order from 1 to 7.

5 Philip baptized the Ethiopian.

2 The Ethiopian was in his chariot reading.

3 Philip sat with the man.

1 Philip met an Ethiopian while he was walking.

6 Philip disappeared.

7 The Ethiopian left rejoicing.

4 Philip explained the good news about Jesus.

Applying God's Word

1. Explain how the prophecy the Ethiopian read was fulfilled in Jesus. (**Jesus humbly and without protest went to the cross to suffer and die for our sins—as a lamb to the slaughter.**)

2. How does this account remind us that salvation by grace through faith in Jesus is for all people? (**The Ethiopian was of a race other than that of the chosen people of God.**)

3. Why was the Ethiopian happy? (**He had come to know Jesus as his Savior.**)

98 Saul's Conversion

(Acts 9)

Thinking about God's Word

1. How did Saul try to get rid of those who believed Christ's doctrine and taught it to others? **(He made out murderous threats against them.)**

2. What happened to Saul on the way to Damascus? **(A light from heaven flashed around him, and he fell to the ground and heard a voice.)**

3. Whose voice was it that spoke to Saul? **(Jesus')** What did He say? **("Saul, Saul, why do you persecute Me?")**

4. Why did Jesus say that Saul was persecuting Him when he had been persecuting the disciples? **(Persecuting Jesus' followers is the same as persecuting Jesus.)**

5. Which words show that Saul's heart was changed toward Jesus? **("At once he began to preach in the synagogues that Jesus is the Son of God.")**

6. With which words did Ananias assure Saul that his sins were forgiven? **("Brother Saul, the Lord Jesus has sent me so that you may see again and be filled with the Holy Spirit.")** How did Saul show that he believed the Lord Jesus was His Savior? **("He got up and was baptized.")**

7. How did Saul now show love instead of hate toward the disciples? **(Saul spent several days with the disciples in Damascus.)** Whose name did he preach instead of blaspheme? **(Jesus')** What did Saul testify of Jesus? **(that Jesus is the Son of God)**

Working with God's Word

Of whom are the following things true?

1. He gave Saul letters to the synagogues in Damascus. **the high priest**

2. He said, "Saul, Saul, why do you persecute Me?" **Jesus**

3. He said, "Who are You, Lord?" **Saul**

4. He came from Tarsus. **Saul**

5. He lived in Damascus. **Ananias**

6. He visited Saul at the Lord's command. **Ananias**

7. He received his sight and was baptized at Damascus. **Saul**

8. They watched the gates of Damascus day and night. **the Jews**

9. They lowered Saul in a basket through an opening in the wall. **his followers**

Draw a line under the word that answers each question correctly.

1. Where did Saul wish to go to persecute Christians? (Samaria—Tarsus—Jerusalem—**Damascus**—Capernaum)

2. What did he plan to do with the Christians he found? (kill them—hang them—send them home—**take them to Jerusalem**)

3. Who spoke to Saul when he fell to the ground? (the soldiers—**Jesus**—Ananias—the high priest)

4. When he got up, what did Saul find out had happened to him? (**He was blind**—There was no one—It was night—He closed his eyes)

5. What was the name of the disciple who lived at Damascus? (Judas—Peter—**Ananias**—Tarsus—John—Andrew)

6. To whom was Saul to bear Jesus' name and His Gospel? (poor people—Samaritans—**Gentiles**—disciples)

7. When the disciple spoke to Saul, what did he call him? (you sinner—poor sinner—Paul—**Brother Saul**—sir)

8. How long was Saul in Damascus? (3 weeks—**several days**—3 days—many years)

9. In whose name did Saul speak when he returned to Jerusalem? (the disciples'—Ananias's—the high priest's—**the Lord's**)

Applying God's Word

1. In what way was Saul persecuting Jesus? **(Saul made murderous threats against the Lord's disciples and sought to take them prisoner.)**

2. Saul was spiritually blind; then he was given sight. Explain. **(God changed Saul from a persecutor of God's people to a great missionary of the Gospel.)**

3. What happened in Saul's life after he became a Christian? **(Saul spent several days with the Lord's disciples in Damascus; then he began to preach and because of it he faced persecution.)**

99 Peter Is Freed from Prison

(Acts 12)

Thinking about God's Word

1. Why was King Herod arresting Christians? **(to persecute them)**
2. Who appeared in the cell? **(an angel)**
3. What happened to Peter's chains? **(They fell off.)**
4. Where did Peter go? **(to the house of Mary the mother of John, also called Mark)**
5. Who answered the door at Mary's house? **(a servant girl name Rhoda)**

Working with God's Word

Fill in the blanks with words from below.

King **Herod** arrested some who belonged to the church. He put **Peter** in prison. Peter would go on trial after the **Passover**. The members of the **church** were praying for Peter. One night an **angel** appeared in Peter's cell. The chains fell off of Peter's **wrists**. Peter followed the **angel** out of prison. Then he went to **Mary's** house. The people did not believe it was **Peter**. When they saw him, they were **astonished**.

church	angel	Passover
Martha's	legs	Peter
astonished	Mary's	Herod
wrists		

Answer each question.

1. Where was Peter put? **in prison**
2. What did the angel tell Peter to do? **"Put on your clothes and sandals. Wrap your cloak around you and follow me."**
3. What did Peter think he was seeing? **a vision**
4. Why did Peter go to Mary's house? **He knew people would be there praying.**
5. What did the believers in Mary's house think was wrong with the servant girl? **They thought she was out of her mind.**
6. What did Peter describe? **how the Lord had brought him out of prison**

Applying God's Word

1. What does this account reveal to us about the role of angels? **(Angels serve and protect the people of God.)**
2. Why is the reaction of the people to Peter's release somewhat unexpected? **(The people were praying for Peter's release, yet they were surprised when Peter arrived among them.)**
3. At the conclusion of the account Peter tells how the Lord rescued him. How might every Christian benefit from Peter's example? **(Each of us can tell others about how God in Christ has rescued us.)**

100 Paul's Shipwreck

(Acts 27–28)

Thinking about God's Word

1. What was the weather like? **(stormy)**

2. Why was the cargo thrown overboard? **(to lighten the load after the ship had received a violent battering)**

3. What did Paul tell the hungry men? **("Last night an angel of the God whose I am and whom I serve stood beside me and said, 'Do not be afraid, Paul. You must stand trial before Caesar; and God has graciously given you the lives of all who sail with you.' So keep up your courage, men, for I have faith in God that it will happen just as He told me.")**

4. Who told Paul not to be afraid? **(an angel)**

5. Where did they decide to run the ship aground? **(an island called Malta)**

6. What were the soldiers going to do with the prisoners? **(kill them)**

7. How many people died in the shipwreck? **(none)**

Working with God's Word

Fill in the blanks with words from below.

1. Paul was sailing to **Italy.**

2. A **storm** swept down from the island.

3. The ship took a violent **battering** from the storm.

4. Neither sun nor **stars** appeared for many days.

5. The men gave up **hope** of being saved.

6. An **angel** appeared to Paul.

7. The angel said all would be **saved.**

8. A **centurion** helped spare Paul's life.

9. The prisoners landed on **Malta.**

10. The islanders were **kind.**

angel	storm	wind
Malta	moon	centurion
Italy	saved	kind
stars	battering	hope

Put these events in order from 1 to 7.

6 Everyone reached land safely.

3 The men gave up hope of being saved.

1 Paul and other prisoners set sail for Italy.

5 The centurion helped Paul stay safe.

4 An angel stood beside Paul.

7 The people of Malta welcomed the men.

2 A wind of hurricane force hit the ship.

Applying God's Word

1. How did God bless Paul's traveling companions because of Paul? **(All who sailed with Paul were spared death in the storm.)**

2. Paul told the sailors that God would save them. To what message of greater salvation had Paul dedicated his life? **(Paul dedicated his life to sharing with all people the Good News of salvation by grace through faith in Jesus.)**

3. Tell how this account from Paul's journeys is a metaphor of the Christian life. **(Jesus, our Savior, promises to remain with us to sustain and encourage us through all the storms of life and finally to take us to live with Him in eternal joy in heaven.)**